BARBIE CASSELMAN'S
Good-for-You Cooking
A HEALTHY-EATING GUIDE

BARBIE CASSELMAN'S

Good-for-You

C·O·O·K·I·N·G

A HEALTHY-EATING GUIDE

Random House
New York, Toronto, London, Sydney, Auckland

Copyright 1993 © Casselman & Company Inc.

All rights reserved under International and Pan American
Copyright Conventions.

Published in Canada in 1993 by Random House of Canada
Limited, Toronto.

Canadian Cataloguing in Publication Data

Casselman, Barbie
    Barbie Casselman's good-for-you cooking

ISBN 0-394-22348-9

1. Cookery.   2. Nutrition.   I. Title.   II. Title: Good-for-you
cooking

TX714.C28 1993a   641.5   C93-093230-7

Photography by Hal Roth Photography Inc.

Design, Art Direction and page composition by Andrew Smith
Graphics Inc.

Printed and bound in Canada

10 9   8   7   6   5   4   3   2   1

COVER PHOTO: *Leek and Lentil Soup (page 155)*

CONTENTS

ACKNOWLEDGEMENTS

WITHOUT THE HELP OF THESE PEOPLE, THIS BOOK WOULD NOT HAVE been written: my husband, Brian, whose hours of research and editing allowed me to keep up with my busy private practice while working on the manuscript; my lawyer, David Himelfarb, and my agent, Linda McKnight; a fabulous publisher, Doug Pepper, and the gang at Random House, who were truly committed to this book; Kerry Barnes, fitness director at Toronto's Adelaide Club, for his patience in discussing exercise physiology; and finally my family and friends for reviewing the manuscript and providing me with their candid comments.

There is one further person to thank, and an important note that accompanies my gratitude. Throughout the book, when mentioning healthy alternatives to convenience foods or recipe ingredients, I recommend President's Choice products, and in several places I suggest using President's Choice Too Good To Be True (TGTBT) foods. I am not advertising for Loblaws and I have not received compensation for these recommendations.

As a nutritionist, I have found President's Choice to be a superior product line. I began recommending it to my clients long before I formed an association with Loblaws to help develop TGTBT products.

I also have great admiration for Dave Nichol, who recognizes the need to provide his customers with convenient, great-tasting products that are also healthy. This marriage between "health food" and tasty convenience foods is a first for Canadian supermarket merchandising. Dave's effort to increase our awareness of what we eat and to help us change our typical North American diet benefits everyone, including our children, nutritionists and our strained health-care system. It makes me proud to be working with him and his team of Unique Product developers.

PREFACE

MY INTEREST IN NUTRITION BEGAN WHEN I WAS A TEENAGER. I WAS five feet two inches tall, small boned, and weighed 135 pounds. I now weigh an even hundred and have remained at this weight for the past 17 years. I have not had a cold or the flu since I was 20. That was 17 years ago! I have the energy to work long days and still enjoy my private life. My first consultation begins at 7:30 a.m. and I work straight through to 4:30, with only a few short breaks. I go to an aerobics class four or five days a week and often on the weekend spend three hours at a stretch cooking.

My metamorphosis was not easy. I had been overweight for quite some time and had tried every diet imaginable. You are probably familiar with several of them. Remember the grapefruit diet? If you ate half a grapefruit before each meal it was supposed to curb your appetite. The way it worked in our family was that the fridge was so full of grapefruit that there was no room for other food.

I tried the Stillman water diet next. I spent so much time running to the bathroom that I had no time to eat! I progressed to Dr. Atkins's high-protein diet and then to Scarsdale. With each new attempt I just got bigger and more depressed.

All the books and articles on nutrition I read only made things worse. Each book contradicted the others, they all required commitment to some method or fad, and my family doctor couldn't explain things to me. Finally, at the age of 19, I went to a nutritionist.

There is an essential difference between what a nutritionist teaches his or her clients and what a growing army of self-made "nutritional experts" push on a naive public. Those advocating fad diets, vitamin and mineral cure-alls and food supplements simply prey on people's confusion and ignorance. They promise that their magic approach is a substitute for sound eating. Coincidentally, they are frequently salespeople with no nutritional education. All too frequently profit is their first motive.

Qualified nutritionists and registered dietitians have passed a four-year course in food and nutrition science at an accredited college or university and have then specialized in a particular area of nutrition. Dietitians must apprentice in a hospital and are policed by an organizational body. Nutritionists continue their education through their own initiative in order to keep their knowledge up to date.

Ethical nutritionists and dietitians do not guarantee results or promise cures. They do not ascribe special health-giving properties to any super-food. They do not recommend an array of expensive vitamins, minerals and food supplements. They emphasize that the nutritional needs of nearly all of us can be met through a balanced diet or with minimal supplementation. However, just as a doctor does not prescribe the same medication to all patients, nutritionists and dietitians do not prescribe the same advice to all clients. A nutritionist or dietitian, like a doctor, must first consider individuals and identify their specific problems. Clients are then taught to modify their attitudes and eating habits.

My nutritionist's personal approach led me to discover that a major change is not something to struggle with on your own — that's like reinventing the wheel. I also came to realize the value of the learning experience and that there are no short cuts to learning properly. Gimmicks and short cuts don't work!

Think about it for a moment. We all know at least one person who has been on a diet — perhaps a revolutionary new diet — or is always on a diet. Forget diets. Dieting doesn't work. The problem is that diets require deprivation — doing without foods you enjoy. So when it comes to diets you're either on or off them. When the diet is over, you return to the way you used to eat. Obviously, the weight you lost is going to come back.

I've counselled nearly 5,000 people from all walks of life. The bottom line is if you don't enjoy particular foods then you're not going to eat them. By learning to enjoy sensible foods you can learn to maintain an appropriate weight and make a significant contribution to your health and well-being — forever. Once you learn to do this you won't even have to think about it. Best of all, you won't have to eat tasteless packaged diet meals or drink diet shakes every day.

But before your behaviour can change, your attitude must change. If you don't make a commitment to learn and practise a better way of eating, your weight will constantly fluctuate as you go on and off your diet. This on-again, off-again or yo-yo dieting syndrome is not to be taken lightly. Every time you gain your weight back, it becomes more difficult to take it off the next time around. Rapid weight gain and loss are also detrimental to your health.

To change your attitude, first consider that healthy eating can be just as much fun as unhealthy eating. I don't expect my clients to give up all the things they like in order to keep their excess weight off. Instead I show them how to make healthy substitutions for the things we all like but that we should avoid. I even have an alternative to french fries (see the recipes on page 236 and 237).

Second, I don't expect anyone to make a commitment to healthy eating out of the blue. You need to know why eating better makes so much sense and how much better it will make you feel. (My clients constantly tell me that they can't get over how great they feel — they never realized the difference could be so noticeable.)

I believe that all of us should be able to feel good without having to resort to drugs or expensive gimmicks. If a new nutritional lifestyle makes you healthier and lets you feel better, perhaps the change will be noticed by those around you. You might encourage others to take better care of themselves — a great start to a more fulfilling life.

An overwhelming number of books provide doubtful and frequently irresponsible promises of better health. In this book I am not offering you a specific diet or miracle program. Nor am I suggesting it as a substitute for regular check-ups by your physician. What I do offer is a no-nonsense user's guide to healthy eating, based on my 14 years of practical experience as a consulting nutritionist. Whether you are a busy executive, a harried homemaker, a yo-yo dieter, a recreational athlete, an older individual who wants to feel much younger or a person who thinks your metabolism is sluggish, this book is for you.

To make the book a user-friendly guide, I have left out the theoretical background. In the first part of the book I have attempted to demystify nutrition. I have also included a range of techniques and tips. I urge you to find which ones work for you.

The second part of the book contains recipes that are tasty and economical. Many can be made ahead and go from the freezer to the microwave. I have included foods that are great to take to work, that provide an alternative to fattening gourmet dishes and that are easy to prepare in quantity and freeze. All the recipes are favourites of mine and of my clients. Healthy food no longer has to taste terrible!

The index serves an important function. Some topics, for example fat and cholesterol, spill over into one another. If you use the index, a thorough review of the practical aspects of any topic is a snap, even if you haven't read the complete text.

Barbie Casselman
November 1992

INTRODUCTION

"YOU ARE ONLY AS OLD AS YOU FEEL." THIS COMMON SAYING IS especially appropriate for our rapidly ageing population. In 1988 about one-third of the North American population was 45 or older, and the percentage has increased since then. By 1996 the oldest baby boomers will turn 50.

Few adults of any age want to look or feel their age, and why should they? With modern science and technology there is no reason we should age nearly as quickly as earlier generations. The billions of dollars devoted to scientific research should keep us not only healthy and vibrant but attractive as well.

Unfortunately, it just doesn't work that way. Along with all of the life-enhancing high-tech developments, we have acquired unhealthy attitudes and habits. We believe that we can defy our biology, and when a part of us breaks or wears out, we assume we can simply have it fixed, replaced or cosmetically made over. But it's not true. We can't defy our biology.

If we want to stay healthy, feel better and look younger, we have to change our lifestyle, by which I mean all the factors that contribute to the way we live our lives: the food we eat, the exercise we get, stress, cigarette and alcohol consumption, our relationships and our spiritual outlook. Yet, even though health professionals are constantly telling us that these factors are important, only rarely do we wake up and change for the better.

For example, in 1990 North Americans spent more than $13 billion on coronary bypass surgery. Yet statistics tell us that within five to seven years, half the bypassed arteries will have clogged up again. Sadly, modern medicine believes that it is acceptable to split people's chests wide open and fool around with their hearts, or subject them to organ transplants, extensive plastic surgery or a lifetime of powerful drugs, despite some pretty terrible side effects. But it is unacceptable to ask people to stop smoking, manage stress more effectively, exercise, eat better and be a little more loving!

It shouldn't take a major disease or disorder for us to appreciate that there is a better way to manage our health and the quality of our lives. But unfortunately we have been conned by advertisers, the press, television stories, movies and product manufacturers who encourage us to believe in the quick fix — instant gratification, instant success, instant meals, fast relief from all symptoms. These promises lead us to choose courses of action that bring only the illusion of accomplishment. Often our choices are barely conscious. We are hypnotized by quick-fix diets and diet pills, mail-order exercise equipment of questionable value, one-step stress management courses and so on. The benefits are short-term and the costs are usually long-term.

The empty promises of consumerism keep us searching for bliss. We waste time and money, and we often sacrifice our health in the quest. We don't develop coping skills or enhance our health, we fall for magic potions, or we treat symptoms without addressing underlying causes. When new symptoms appear, we are quick to get rid of them, again failing to solve the real problem. If one gimmick doesn't work, we are ready to believe in the next one that comes along. Maybe it's because the promise sounds better, perhaps because the package is more attractive or because only "four small payments" are required.

Our work-hard, play-hard approach culminated in the unofficial call of the 1980s, "Work until you drop." If a problem develops, take a pill to block the symptoms or get the doctor to fix you so you can get back at it again. Now people as young as 30 or 40 are suffering from heart problems, cancer and other diseases we thought only older people got. Initially, such unfortunate outcomes did not seem to have apparent causes. Yet, as these exceptions became commonplace, we came to accept them. We even found a name for them: "lifestyle disorders."

By giving labels to causes of major suffering and premature death, we gave them legitimacy. We took a casual attitude toward them and accepted them as a part of life. Well, they are not legitimate. They usually tell us that something is wrong with the way we live. We cannot expect to lead healthy and productive lives if we make a habit of rushing to the local burger joint between business meetings for greasy meat between two slices of white dough, then feed the kids hot dogs and Cokes. We can't chain-smoke and drink five or 10 coffees a day. Every time we get the urge to exercise we can't lie down until it goes away. And fruit is not an experience to save for old age!

The attitude of "don't worry, be happy" just doesn't cut it anymore. Now is the time to worry — although I don't mean we should scare ourselves. I mean that we should not take for granted the myths our society sells us each day. Some of us try to lead healthy lives, but even when we try to follow sensible guidelines we frequently are fooled. When it comes to nutrition information, for example, inaccuracy and confusion reign supreme. Consider labels that say "cholesterol-free." What some manufacturers conveniently don't tell us is that lots of "cholesterol-free" foods, such as peanut butter, potato chips and mayonnaise, are loaded with fats, which are a major contributor to high cholesterol.

Healthy nutrition means not taking mainstream information at face value. But before you can make informed assessments, you have to understand the principles of proper nutrition. The process of learning such principles is no different from the process of learning anything else. Compare it to swinging a golf club or a tennis racquet. Once you have reviewed and practised the individual steps, carrying out the action — the swing — eventually becomes an unconscious act, and you no longer have to think of each step involved. Your mind is free to concentrate on other things.

However, a healthy lifestyle is not simply a matter of forcing down a bowl of oat bran or some tofu, or occasionally reading labels, although these all contribute. New behaviour must be practised consistently. Habits develop slowly, but if learned properly, through practice they become second nature. Through initial effort and a little experimenting, your tastes and preferences will also change over time.

My clients frequently tell me after they have eaten healthier foods for a month or two that the rich, fattening dishes they used to enjoy seem heavy and hard to digest. Their bodies naturally adjust to lighter choices. For example, many begin to prefer 1% or 2% milk to cream in their coffee.

There is one key point here that we miss so often: although your new nutritional habits will become second nature, it does not mean you will never have to give nutrition a second thought.

For example, have you ever noticed that the best athletes are not necessarily the most talented but are the ones willing to review and drill the basics forever? It's this practice that allows them to have that superior performance in a clinch.

When you compare my approach to the "quick-fix" diet alternatives, it's easy to see why they don't work in the long run. Such diets simply restrict your choices. You don't develop skills to get you through tough times. You're stuck when dining out, when travelling, when you can't mix up an instant diet drink, or in any other situation in which the rules don't apply. In my approach there are no inflexible rules to follow. When you develop a skill, your responses to a challenge become very flexible. For example, minimizing the damage is a key component of my approach. We're all human and we all overeat from time to time, or we find ourselves at a dinner with a set menu. I don't chastise my clients for indulgence in these situations. I teach them to deal with such temptations and restrictions in a constructive fashion so that a one-time exception doesn't lead to guilt and blowing the whole effort. Through practice, they develop an array of choices that help them to cope without aggravation.

THE BENEFITS OF A NUTRITIONAL LIFESTYLE

Proper nutrition and weight control are the starting points to feeling good, and to feeling good *about* ourselves. And feeling good is the biggest part of everything we do. If we don't feel good and feel good about ourselves, we can't feel good about the world around us and about our actions in that world. In short, we can't be happy. Because proper nutrition puts the body in a condition that allows us to feel good, it really is a key component of health and well-being. The heightened sense of self-esteem, motivation and energy experienced by those who eat well is well documented. Focusing on the job at hand, dealing with difficult situations, and maintaining a positive mental attitude become that much easier when we eat properly.

I'm sure most of you at least once were too busy in the morning for breakfast, so you grabbed a coffee and maybe a Danish. You got a quick rush from the caffeine and sugar, blasted through the first hour or so and then crashed. So you had another coffee to hold you till lunch. Then more coffee with lunch and at three or four o'clock you really crashed. By the time the day was over you were so exhausted and frazzled that you didn't feel like exercising, and you ended up taking out your aggravation on someone you care about.

To a greater or lesser extent this destructive routine plagues most of us. Because we eat badly, we don't feel well, and we again eat poorly in order to cheer ourselves up. Poor nutrition not only affects our moods but also contributes to many health-related problems that we can no longer afford to deny.

Remember the stories you heard of people who led abusive lifestyles living into their 90s? These are the rare exceptions! Unfortunately, those who take care of themselves do sometimes become seriously ill or die before their time. However, if such people didn't watch their health, they might have developed health problems 10 or more years earlier. The point is to not play Russian roulette with your health. The odds are heavily against you.

Consider the disorders poor nutrition contributes to. An unhealthy diet plays a significant role in breast, colon and stomach cancers and in several digestive disorders. Adult-onset diabetes, arthritis and backaches are all much more commonly experienced by overweight people. Poor eaters are more likely to suffer from colds and flu, depression and sleeping problems. A proper diet reduces the incidence and severity of these problems, and even makes our hair, nails and skin look healthier.

Overweight people and unhealthy eaters take an average of 85% longer to recover in hospital. Those who are overweight suffer a greater risk of heart disease and high blood pressure. Yet, with a proper diet, the risk of coronary disease decreases significantly. And many people on prescriptions for high blood pressure can (with medical supervision) cut back or cease taking medication altogether, thereby eliminating costly drugs that often have side effects such as extreme fatigue and lethargy.

From a psychological perspective, unhealthy eating serves as a crutch that helps us when we are under stress or depressed. How often do you think, "Of course I'm under stress, but it's nothing a chocolate bar can't fix"? Perhaps you gulp your food without tasting it or get up in the middle of the night to eat a snack. Now,

I know that for some people eating in the middle of the night may be fun, but food isn't digested properly when we sleep. Many people wake up in the morning feeling lethargic, depressed or bloated, or they have acid indigestion. It's not a pleasant way to start the day and it adversely affects everything we do.

Proper nutrition, on the other hand, has enormous benefits:

- It provides the energy to exercise and stimulates our motivation to maintain a fitness regimen.
- It minimizes the effects of nicotine withdrawal and helps to prevent weight gain when we quit smoking.
- It helps to strengthen our body's immune system — our natural defence system that fights disease and the effects of stress.
- By learning good nutritional habits, we acquire skills that help us in other areas of our life.

My corporate clients can testify to one further point — proper nutrition not only improves health but saves money. Preventive health programs help to reduce absenteeism and other health-related costs, enhance employees' energy and improve their focus and work capacity. In our competitive environment, this translates into significantly increased productivity.

Part I
WHAT DO YOU THINK YOU'RE EATING EVERY DAY?

THE THREE CS ARE BECOMING MORE ORGANIZED AND MORE VOCAL. Who are the Three Cs? They are people who are concerned, caring and conscientious about their health. They are the consumers who shop for healthier foods, order their salad dressing on the side and aren't grossed out by tofu. They fully appreciate the importance of preventative health programs and know that happiness comes from enjoying their vices in moderation.

But they are still the minority. Did you know that nearly three-quarters of North Americans still prefer soft white bread to whole grain bread? And the preference for this intestinal glue remains in spite of all the press that fibre has received during the past several years. Additionally, in the last century we have increased our protein and fat consumption by about 30% and we eat twice the sugar we used to. But we eat only about half the complex carbohydrates that our ancestors did, and we have reduced our daily intake of fibre by 70 to 80%. It's no wonder 35 to 40% of us could stand to lose some weight.

Consider also that we have become sedentary but have not significantly reduced our intake of calories. And demands for convenience have resulted in a considerable reduction in the nutritive value of our food. Given such easy access to thousands of packaged convenience foods, we eat more calories than we should but receive fewer nutrients than ever before!

The "typical North American diet" did not evolve from a need for health. As we became more affluent, we demanded more convenience foods and increasing amounts of red meat. The food industry responded to our demands, and as competition for new and tastier products grew, so did nutritional sacrifices. Just as we never considered the risks of cigarette smoking, air pollution or a host of prescription drugs, we never considered the risks of a radical departure from our traditional diet. Besides, each of us individually makes the choice to live on convenience food. No one ever told us to cut out unprocessed, natural food sources.

In contrast, history clearly indicates that most of humankind, over much of its evolution, has subsisted on near-vegetarian diets, and the majority of the world still lives that way. But don't get me wrong — never for a moment am I saying that we should all revert to vegetarianism. However, in what follows I will dispel the myths and explain why it is essential to modify our typical diets. I will also show you how to make intelligent substitutions for the junk foods that we typically eat.

Chapter 1
SEPARATING FAT
FROM FICTION

FAT CONSUMPTION IS KEY WHEN IT COMES TO MAINTAINING A HEALTHY body weight, an acceptable cholesterol level and optimum health. The amount of fat we eat often plays a larger role in our weight than the number of calories we consume. And the amount and type of fats in our diet directly affects our risk of developing several diseases — including heart disease, which accounts for 50% of deaths in North America — and a variety of cancers and digestive disorders.

Several topics need to be addressed when it comes to fat. These are: fat as it relates to metabolism and weight loss; the kinds and sources of fat in our diet; the role of fat in our cholesterol level; and the benefits of exercise in reducing body fat. Let's consider these issues one at a time.

THE FAT YOU EAT IS THE FAT YOU WEAR: FAT AND METABOLISM

North Americans currently eat more fat than ever before — too much fat. One tablespoon of fat per day, consumed in an otherwise healthy diet, satisfies our total fat demand. At the outside, we should ingest no more than 30% of our total calories from fat, but fat often totals 40 to 50% of our daily caloric intake.

This does not mean that you can consume an unlimited amount of proteins and carbohydrates, as excess consumption of these foods will also be stored as fat. The point is that our bodies need more protein and carbohydrate than fat for fuel and tissue regeneration, so we use calories from these sources more efficiently. The proper ratio is 15% protein, 55% carbohydrate and 30% fat.

Fat is the most easily stored food source, and — couch potatoes take note — it does not burn off without physical effort. Some overweight people complain that they don't eat all that much, and they may not. Our bodies need so little fat for proper functioning that 97% of all fat calories consumed in our typical high-fat diets are converted into body fat. So even those of us who don't eat a lot of calories often become overweight.

The problem with fat is that it's more calorically dense than proteins and carbohydrates: fat has a lot more calories per gram than do proteins and carbohydrates. (A gram of fat has nine calories; a gram of protein or carbohydrate has only four calories.) Fat does not necessarily fill you up as much as carbohydrates or proteins. One tablespoon of oil in your salad dressing has 125 calories. Two pieces of bread have about the same. Which fills you up the most? The bread, of course. It's easy to eat a tremendous amount of fat, consuming twice the calories, and not fill up as much as if you ate a complex carbohydrate like pasta or grain.

If you are trying to lose weight and eat too much fat, even if your total caloric intake is low, the process of mobilizing your body fat to meet energy needs will slow or stop. Also, the action of digestion burns only 5% of the calories consumed from fat, whereas it burns about 20% of the calories from proteins and carbohydrates. No matter how you look at it — fat makes you fat!

DIETARY SOURCES OF FAT

We eat three types of fat: saturated, monounsaturated and polyunsaturated. (The names refer to their chemical structure.) Each fat has different effects on the body. Although research accepts that two of them are good for us, they are beneficial only when eaten in moderation.

Saturated Fats

Fat and oils are the same substance, differing only in consistency. Saturated fats are solid at room temperature and turn to oil when heated; lard, shortening, butter and the marbling in steak are examples. Unsaturated fats, on the other hand, are liquid at room temperature and take the form of oil.

Although we are just beginning to learn about the role of fat in our health, there is clearly enough evidence to warrant a restricted intake of all sources of fat. Our consumption of saturated fat is a major concern, because saturated fat is the most unhealthy type of fat. It raises our cholesterol and triglyceride (the storage form of fat) levels. It also seems to interfere with immune functioning. (Our immune system fights against illness and diseases, ranging from common colds to cancer.) Well-documented studies show that those who eat low-fat diets have a measurable increase in their immune functioning, with much less incidence of heart disease and some cancers.

Most saturated fats come from animal sources. The exceptions are coconut, palm and palm kernel oils. Although these vegetable oils are liquid at room temperature, they contain mostly saturated fat. In fact, they are often called saturated fats instead of oils.

Coconut and palm oil are the fats we find in so many processed and prepared foods, from crackers and cookies to frozen dinners. If a label says that a product "may contain" one of these oils, it probably does. Sometimes a label says "contains vegetable oils" so as not to draw our attention to the kind of fat used. If manufacturers use healthy vegetable oil, you can be sure they will clearly list it.

Monounsaturated Fats

Monounsaturated fats are liquid at room temperature, and we know them as oils. Although some are called monounsaturated, all oils contain all three kinds of fat. The chart on page 26 shows the ratios of the different kinds of fat in each oil. Olive oil, peanut oil and canola oil, for example, are "monounsaturated" because they have more monounsaturated fat in them than they have saturated or polyunsaturated fat. Canola oil is the best choice of these three, as it contains the least amount of saturated fat. Oils that are high in monounsaturated fat are the healthiest type of oils, as they help to increase the "good" cholesterol, called HDL.

Polyunsaturated Fats

Polyunsaturated fats are also liquid at room temperature. These fats come from plant sources. Examples are sunflower oil (69% polyunsaturated), safflower oil (78%), soybean oil (61%) and corn oil (62%). These are the second healthiest type of fat because they help lower total cholesterol and triglycerides. Triglycerides are the storage form of fat, and elevated levels often signal a diet that is too rich in fat. However, polyunsaturated fats also slightly lower the HDL, or "good," cholesterol. (They were considered the healthiest type of fat before we became aware of their HDL-lowering quality.) The following chart simplifies the issue of healthy fat.

FAT COMPOSITION OF OILS

	Saturated	Monounsaturated	Polyunsaturated
Butterfat	66%	30%	4%
Canola Oil	6	58	36
Coconut Oil	92	6	2
Corn Oil	13	25	62
Cotton Seed Oil	27	19	54
Lard	41	47	12
Olive Oil	14	77	9
Peanut Oil	18	48	34
Palm Oil	51	39	10
Safflower Oil	9	13	78
Sesame Oil	15	40	45
Soybean Oil	15	24	61
Sunflower Oil	11	20	69

The oils in the chart can be assigned a health rating. Higher ratings are a combination of low saturated fat content and high monounsaturated fat content. From most healthy to least healthy, the list is: canola, olive, safflower, sunflower, sesame, peanut, corn, soybean and cottonseed. Lard, palm oil, butter and coconut oil are considered unhealthy.

Hydrogenated Oil

There is one more type of oil — hydrogenated oil. Hydrogenation is the process of adding hydrogen atoms to fat; this process changes polyunsaturated fat into saturated fat. That's right, a healthy fat is changed into an unhealthy fat. Even worse, low-cost oils, such as palm kernel oil, which is already saturated, may be used. Again, a nutritional trick that produces profit for food manufacturers.

The hydrogenated oils give products longer shelf lives, as the oil is less likely to break down and become rancid. This is why some packaged cookies can sit on the shelf for a few months, but homemade cookies go stale quickly. Hydrogenated oils are solid at room temperature. For example, the hydrogenated oil in commercial peanut butter doesn't float on the surface like the oil in natural peanut butter, and margarine is solid for spreading on bread. Manufacturers assume that hydrogenation makes foods more appealing to us. By the way, don't fry with margarine. The application of heat changes the fat in margarine into a form similar to saturated fat.

Many commercially prepared foods, like french fries and doughnuts, are often fried in hydrogenated oil because the oil can be heated to a very high temperature before it smokes. This allows food to be cooked quickly, and the oil can also be reused many times. In contrast, healthy oil has to be discarded after a few uses.

Packaged foods such as cookies, crackers, sauces, snack foods and "light" meals frequently contain hydrogenated oil. Even dietetic foods often contain it. This is one reason we rarely hear that diet foods are healthy, only that they have fewer calories. Remember, "diet" and "health" are frequently contradictory terms.

Common Sources of Hidden Fat

Since product manufacturers try to downplay the fat content of many foods, we are often not aware of the fat that hides in the foods we eat. Let's look at some major sources of dietary fat to see why it's easy to unknowingly consume up to three-quarters of our daily calories in fat:

- The greatest source of hidden fat is salad dressing. And a Caesar salad is the worst culprit, as it might contain bacon and fried croutons. You may think a large Caesar salad is the healthiest thing on the lunch menu, but it weighs in at about 650 calories, and about 90% of those calories come from fat. A Caesar salad is a worse choice than a smoked meat sandwich!
- I'm sorry to break the news to you about this next item — the commercially made muffin. A large muffin contains 400 to 500

calories, and typically 70% of them come from fat. This is more fat than in a chocolate cream-filled doughnut. But that doesn't mean you can eat the doughnut. It's full of hydrogenated oil, too. Look for low-fat muffins, or packaged muffins that use water instead of oil — or make your own and freeze them. (See my recipes on pages 251, 252 and 253.) Try replacing dough-nuts with whole grain toast sprinkled with cinnamon and a lit-tle Splenda brand sweetener.

- Many foods are not fattening themselves; it's what we put on top that's fattening. A medium-sized baked potato has only 140 calories, but three (level) tablespoons of sour cream add 90 calories, mostly of saturated fat. The same potato made into potato chips is fried in oil, adding 300 calories from fat.
- The common characteristic of nuts, seeds and olives is that they can be turned to oil, which is fat. Nuts seem innocent, but just half a cup, the equivalent of a few handfuls, has more than 500 high-fat calories. Sunflower and sesame seeds are also high in fat, as are olives.

FAT AND CHOLESTEROL

Cholesterol is a white, waxy, fat-like substance that exists natu-rally in the body. It's important to many processes, including the formation of sex hormones, nerve cell function and vitamin D synthesis. Not all the cholesterol in your body comes from food: some is produced by your liver. Cholesterol is manufactured only by the livers of animals, so animal protein is the only source of cholesterol. However, some animal flesh is lower in cholesterol and saturated fat than others.

High blood cholesterol is a silent killer. A heart attack or stroke may be the first indication that something is wrong. However, your cholesterol level is not difficult to monitor and control. The major factors for those with high blood cholesterol are the amount of saturated fat that they eat and the amount of total fat consumed each day. It is not, as we are often led to believe, the amount of cholesterol in their diet. Let me explain.

The liver both makes and clears away cholesterol. Excess con-sumption of saturated fat reduces the liver's ability to clear choles-terol from the bloodstream. But by making the right food choices, most people can reduce their fat intake enough to lower blood cholesterol by up to 30% in just three weeks! The relationship between dietary cholesterol (the amount of cholesterol we eat) and blood cholesterol is not as clear. For this reason food products advertised as cholesterol-free (and good for you) are not always safe to eat. These foods are frequently high in fat. If you avoid such products, rather than worry about eating an egg here or there, you'll be much further ahead.

Even if you did not eat any cholesterol, your body could manufacture sufficient amounts. A feedback mechanism regulates your cholesterol level. When it's low, the liver produces more, and when it's high, which occurs when you eat too much fat and cholesterol, the liver responds by shutting down production. However, the decrease in production is not enough to compensate for the amounts of fat and cholesterol that many of us consume.

Unfortunately, some people have cholesterol feedback mechanisms that do not work properly. If these people eat even a moderate amount of fat and cholesterol, they are prone to heart disease early in life. Some people with normal feedback mechanisms who eat too much fat are also prone to high cholesterol. On the other hand, a few lucky people are highly immune to heart disease. It's not, however, a good idea to bet on which group you fall into, as a high-fat, high-cholesterol diet contributes to more health problems than just heart disease.

There are two types of cholesterol, LDL and HDL. The bad cholesterol, LDL, transports excess cholesterol to your arteries, where it builds up like a wax on the artery walls. This build-up causes arteries to narrow, a problem commonly referred to as "hardening of the arteries." The resulting constriction raises blood pressure, causing a variety of problems, and can cut off blood flow to the heart or brain, resulting in a heart attack or stroke. The good cholesterol, HDL, clears cholesterol from your arteries and takes it back to the liver for reprocessing or excretion.

A normal cholesterol reading, after fasting for 12 to 14 hours, is 3.6 to 6.2 (in Canadian units). A level between 5.2 and 6.2 is borderline high.

To eliminate the possibility of cholesterol-induced artery blockage, current Canadian medical guidelines say that you should maintain a level below 5.0. However, populations the world over who eat very little fat and have very low cholesterol levels rarely suffer from heart disease.

The HDL/LDL ratio is also important because if, for example, your total cholesterol is high and your HDL component is low, your risk of a heart attack can be much higher than the risk of a person with normal ratios. The ratio of HDL to total cholesterol should be at least 20%. The findings of several independent researchers should provide encouragement for people with cholesterol problems. The distinguished cardiologist Dr. Dean Ornish, among others, has proven that people with seriously blocked arteries can reopen them when they reduce their blood cholesterol levels by following Ornish's recommendations. (In addition to nutritional modification he recommends regular aerobic exercise and other lifestyle changes.)

Since present North American guidelines for acceptable daily cholesterol intake are a subject of debate and may turn out to be too lenient, it is sensible to minimize our consumption of fat and cholesterol. When eating a balanced diet, you will never consume too little of either for good health. Finally, as the typical North American diet contributes to arterial blockage almost from birth onward, if you have a family history of heart disease, monitor your children's cholesterol levels as well as your own.

How to Reduce the Cholesterol and Fat in Your Diet

- For those of you who like shrimp, the good news is that it's no longer restricted on low-cholesterol diets and may be eaten in moderation. Shrimp has little saturated fat, is high in omega-3 fatty acids and has been shown to help lower total cholesterol.
- Eat more fish and seafood if you have been avoiding them. Salmon, mackerel and many shellfish such as lobster, crab, mussels and scallops are rich in omega-3 fatty acids and low in saturated fat, and therefore are very healthy.
- Reduce your consumption of fatty meat. Fatty meat does not have more cholesterol than lean meat, but fattier cuts contribute to high cholesterol levels, as they contain more saturated fat.
- Avoid or minimize consumption of organ meats such as liver, kidney, heart, brains and sweetbreads, which are extremely high in cholesterol.

- Reduce your consumption of egg yolks, as they are high in cholesterol. The yolk of one large egg contains all the cholesterol that you should consume in a day. If you like eggs, try scrambled eggs or omelettes made from three whites and one yolk.
- Eat less food, but more often. Recent findings at the University of Toronto show that eating six small meals a day lowers blood cholesterol more effectively that eating one or two large meals. This regimen would be useful for those who have dangerously high cholesterol levels.

Cholesterol-lowering drugs have some immediate side effects, such as nausea, constipation, gas and bloating. We do not yet know their long-term effects. Dietary alternatives are far more pleasant and healthy.

Your total fat intake should be limited to 30% of the total calories you consume, and saturated fat should be no more than 10% of your total caloric intake. LDL (bad) cholesterol levels will continue to decrease as you remove saturated fat from your diet. The following formula is useful when reviewing your consumption of fat. Say, for example, you eat 2,000 calories per day and you want to know the maximum amount of fat you should eat:

30% x 2,000 = 600 calories
You can eat up to 600 fat calories.

There are 9 calories in every gram of fat, so you can eat 600÷9 or 67 grams of fat each day. No more than one-third of these calories should be saturated fat, so you can eat 22 grams of saturated fat per day. These suggestions will easily allow you to follow the recommendations:

- Reduce your consumption of animal protein to 6 ounces a day. Make meat a side dish instead of an entree, or try one of my stir-fry recipes (see pages 190 or 202). Eat pasta, rice, potatoes, grains, vegetables and legumes as main courses. (Some of these complex carbohydrates are also good sources of protein.)
- Use leaner cuts of meat and marinate them to tenderize and add flavour.

- Remove the skin from poultry. Eat only the white meat, which is leaner than dark meat. Small chickens, turkeys and Cornish game hens are the leanest poultry. Small chickens are less than 10% fat, but large hens are 20 to 30% fat.
- Try ground turkey or chicken (without the skin) instead of beef for burgers, chili and meat sauces. (Make sure to keep all fowl properly refrigerated and wash all cooking utensils, dishes and countertops carefully after each use.)
- If you like wild game, pheasant, wild duck, rabbit, quail and venison are lean. Avoid goose, capon and farm-raised duck.
- Drink skim milk or 1% milk.
- Buy plain, no-fat yogurt, add your own fruit or a teaspoon of President's Choice Twice the Fruit jam, or "all fruit" jam found in health food stores and some supermarkets. You can also use the jams on toast, and leave off the butter. This reduces both fat and sugar consumption.
- Choose healthy oils from the chart on page 26. As much as possible, use monounsaturated oils such as canola oil. Strong-flavoured oils, like sesame and olive oil, are also good choices as you don't need a lot to impart the flavour.
- Sherbet, frozen yogurt, Rice Dream, Tofutti Lite and so on are low-fat (but not always low-cal) alternatives to ice cream. Some low-calorie alternatives are Gise, light Fudgsicles and light Creamsicles. When possible, check labels for fat and sugar content.
- Replace fattening foods with complex carbohydrates, which are filling, full of nutrients and higher in fibre. Over time, you will find that you lose your taste for rich, fattening foods.
- Eat whole grain breads. They are more flavourful than refined white bread and don't need butter or margarine to taste good.
- Commercially baked goods, for example pie crusts and croissants, are high in saturated fat and best avoided. Look for products made with reasonable amounts of polyunsaturated or monounsaturated oil.
- Non-dairy coffee whiteners, almost all fat, should be avoided.
- Be on the lookout for new fat-free and low-fat products that are now sharing shelf-space with traditional favourites. Exciting new foods are emerging almost weekly.

- For low-fat cooking, roast, bake, grill, broil or barbecue.
- Don't fry. Use non-stick cookware and a light coating of environmentally friendly cooking spray instead of oil or butter. Non-stick woks need very little oil.
- Let homemade soups cool, remove the fat when they are cold, and then reheat to serve.
- Make sauces by adding stock or broth to pan juices after removing the fat. Thicken by boiling rapidly for a few minutes, and flavour with herbs and spices.
- Use buttermilk in cooking. Surprisingly, it's low in fat.
- Sauté onions in water, not oil.
- In dips, use no-fat yogurt instead of sour cream or mayonnaise.
- Top potatoes and vegetables with Dijon mustard, vegetable based dips, Molly McButter or yogurt instead of butter or sour cream.
- Instead of butter, season vegetables with herbs, lemon juice or stock.
- Become more familiar with your microwave. Use it to cook and reheat food and do without the oil or butter.
- There are several new low-fat cheeses available and many are suitable for cooking. Some taste identical to the high-fat versions, and most deli counters will let you taste before buying.

FAT AND EXERCISE

Exercise such as walking, cycling and cross-country skiing uses the body's major muscles. When we do these activities for more than a few minutes, our muscles require large amounts of oxygen in order to burn fuel (protein, carbohydrates and fat). Given the role of oxygen in burning fuel, these exercises are called *aerobic* exercises. Regular aerobic exercise helps us lose weight, and weight loss helps reduce cholesterol levels. Aerobic exercise also helps raise HDL (good) cholesterol.

Although exercise helps normalize cholesterol, it's better if you don't smoke, as smoking contributes to the accumulation of fatty deposits on the arterial walls, which causes them to narrow. And dealing effectively with stress lowers the liver's cholesterol production.

How to Burn Fat While Exercising

Aerobic exercise comprises three elements: frequency, duration and intensity. A different combination of these three components is required for the combined goals of aerobic fitness and fat burning than for a strictly aerobic or cardiovascular benefit. Try to apply the following considerations to maximize the benefits derived from your own fitness routine.

If you exercise regularly, say five times a week, your body burns a larger amount of fat *for the same amount of exercise* than if you were to *exercise less frequently*. Exercising three times a week burns only a minimal amount of fat. Four times is better, and five times best, although hard to fit into most schedules.

Numerous studies have proven that in addition to regular exercise, aerobic exercise of consistant, moderate intensity aids fat burning. For example, strolling as opposed to fast walking, although continuous, is not intense enough to facilitate fat burning (but it does help to raise HDL cholesterol). Interval training of any type, such as a sprint-walk combination, is not of consistant, moderate intensity, and therefore is not an efficient fat burner. And high-impact aerobics is too intense for a beginner to efficiently burn fat.

The goal of weight maintenance or *healthy* weight loss is to burn fat, not lean muscle tissue. Aerobic exercise that raises your heart rate to moderate intensity levels (60 to 70% of aerobic maximum) for more than 20 minutes — ideally 30 to 60 minutes — burns fat most efficiently while minimizing lean muscle loss. However, when exercising, our bodies never burn fat alone. We burn fat, protein and carbohydrate in ever-changing ratios.

Our bodies convert the carbohydrates we eat into glycogen, which is stored to meet our energy demands. After 20 to 30 minutes of moderately intense, continuous and consistent exercise, our glycogen stores start to be reduced. At the same time, if we oxygenate our tissues effectively, they use fat in addition to glycogen for fuel. However, when the exercise intensity approaches our anaerobic threshold (about 80% of aerobic maximum for the average exerciser, or the level at which we can no longer comfortably carry on a conversation), the number of calories supplied from fat decreases considerably. At this intensity, oxygen cannot be supplied to the body fast enough to burn fat.

Age, weight, sex and genetic makeup determine the number of calories we burn and the amounts that come from fat and glycogen. As exercise intensity increases, the consumption ratios of fat to glycogen vary tremendously from one person to the next. Generally, those in better aerobic shape will burn a greater ratio of fat to glycogen than people who are not as aerobically fit. (For these reasons, when "fat-burning" books and courses tell you exactly how much fat you will lose by following their exercise program, you should not accept the numbers at face value.)

For illustrative purposes, a typical, fit, 180-pound, 30-year-old male burns anywhere from 50 to 100% more *total* calories when jogging than when walking for the same period. However, these calories are not necessarily fat calories, as the greater-intensity exercise favours carbohydrates (glycogen) as fuel. This is why walking is an efficient fat-burning exercise.

If you push yourself to an extreme and try to lose weight through high intensity or too frequent exercise, you will start to burn the protein stored in lean muscle tissue for fuel. This will cause muscles to break down. The objective is to exercise in order to retain and build lean muscle tissue and lose fat. You only fool yourself by exercising too hard.

On the other hand, if you crash diet and do not exercise, up to 30% of initial weight loss can be from lost muscle because, in this situation, your body also consumes the protein stored in your muscles for fuel. This explains why so many dieters look gaunt and have loose skin. Exercise tones and trims you. You look better even before you reach your target weight.

Exercise also enables you to more easily keep the unwanted pounds from sneaking back, because it builds muscle tissue. Muscle tissue is more metabolically active than fat — it burns more calories at rest than does fat. An average-sized person burns 70 calories per hour at rest. If physically fit, the same person burns up to 10 more calories per hour, or over 14% more calories. Over a year this is a considerable amount of increased fat burning.

Just How Effective Is a Low-Fat Diet When Combined with Walking As a Fat-Burning Exercise?

Common nutritional wisdom says that for every 3,500 calories you burn you will lose one pound. Although it takes 3,500 calories to make one pound, you do not lose one pound *of fat* simply by burning 3,500 calories. During medium-intensity walking you will burn up to a 50/50 mixture of carbohydrate (glycogen) and fat. So, if you walk for an hour each day and burn 300 calories, you will burn a maximum of 150 fat calories. This, however, adds up to 1,050 calories from fat, or almost one third of a pound of fat per week!

If you eat a better diet that includes less fat, you can easily eliminate about 2,100 fat calories each week. Add these to the 1,050 calories you burn walking one hour each day, and you will have a fat calorie deficit of 3,150, or a little less than one pound of fat each week.

As I mentioned, more intense exercise, like jogging, burns more glycogen than does walking; and glycogen reserves act as a sensor for appetite stimulation. So the more glycogen you burn, the hungrier you get. The result — walking burns two-thirds or more of the fat calories that are burned while jogging, but stimulates your appetite much less.

It is important to try to eat within 90 minutes after exercising, as your body needs the nutrients for tissue repair. The food also prevents you from becoming ravenously hungry and bingeing later. If you eat a low-fat, high-carbohydrate meal, you will replace the glycogen but not the fat. Even if you eat a bit too much, you will not gain back fat as readily, because within two hours of exercising, your body will store most of the extra carbohydrate calories as glycogen and not as fat. But don't eat a big meal before going for a fat-burning walk. Walking after a high-carbohydrate meal will minimize fat burning and maximize carbohydrate burning.

How Many Calories Should I Eat Each Day and How Many of These Should Come from Fat?

The following guide considers your activity level to let you find the approximate number of calories that you should eat each day and the number of those calories that should come from fat. First determine your energy factor as follows:

10. Very Sedentary: Mostly sitting at a desk or confined to the home or to a few rooms. Slow walking but no running.
11. Sedentary: Walking or some slow jogging are your main activ-

ities, but less than 10 minutes of continuous running a week. Recreation includes bowling, fishing, snowmobiling, boating and similar activities.

12. Moderately Active: Golfing 18 holes, doubles tennis, sailing, pleasure swimming or skating, downhill skiing, and similar activity. Also, 10 to 20 minutes of continuous running (at your target heart rate) at least three times a week.

13. Active: Jogging, swimming, competitive tennis, cross-country skiing and the like, for more than 20 continuous minutes, more than three times a week. Or similar activity at a recreational pace for more than 45 minutes at least three times a week.

14. Very Active: At least 90 minutes of vigorous activity four days a week. For example, training for competitive athletics, full-court basketball, weight training, football or wrestling. Or more than 2.5 hours of recreational activity four or more times a week.

15. Super Active: The activity level in 14 plus an active or physical job.

Multiply your desired weight by your energy factor. Realize, however, the weight that is *healthiest* for you to maintain and your *desired* weight may not be identical, as many of us frequently aspire to be slimmer than we should be. Please use question seven on page 115 to decide your ideal weight before continuing.

Now multiply your desired weight by your energy factor to find the number of calories to consume daily to maintain your desired weight. Then multiply the number of calories you need to eat by 0.3 to find the number of those calories that should be consumed from fat, and multiply total caloric intake by 0.1 to determine your saturated fat allowance.

For example, if you are moderately active your energy factor is 12. Say that you want to weigh 150 pounds. You can consume 1,800 calories per day (12 x 150 = 1,800). Your fat calorie allowance = 1,800 x 0.3 or 540. (To find the number of *grams* that can come from fat, divide the number of calories by 9; 540÷9 = 60 grams of fat.) Calories from saturated fat = 1,800 x 0.1 = 180. Therefore, 180 calories can come from saturated fat. And 180÷9

= 20, so 20 grams of *saturated* fat are allowed daily. Remember, when calculating fat consumption, the number you get is the maximum recommended; a bit less is better.

This formula serves as a rough guide to caloric intake. Let your bathroom scale be the final indicator. If you want to be precise, weigh yourself at the *same* time of day on the *same* balance scale. The weight of a large person can fluctuate by four pounds over 24 hours. Also, the accuracy of common bathroom scales can vary by two to three pounds. By using the same scale you will have a consistent reference point. To summarize:

• Walking one hour a day, five times a week, burns about 1,500 calories a week, and about 750 of these come from fat.
• A low-fat diet, as opposed to the typical North American diet, can reduce fat consumption by about 2,100 calories each week.
• The combined *fat* deficit from walking and a low-fat diet is 2,850 fat calories per week, or about ¾ of a pound of fat.
• By increasing muscle tone, regular aerobic exercise raises total caloric demand about 14%, or 1,650 calories a week for the average person.
• As you will see later, those who regularly drink alcohol consume about 1,000 to 1,500 additional empty calories every week from the alcohol — and this doesn't include calories from the snack foods that so often accompany the drinks.

Most people have never considered exactly how fattening it is to sit around, drink alcohol, and eat a high-fat diet: someone eating the typical North American diet who drinks regularly will consume an average of 3,100 to 3,600 calories each week more (2,100 fat calories plus 1,000 to 1,500 alcohol calories) than a moderate drinker who eats a low-fat diet. A sedentary drinker also expends fewer calories per week than someone who exercises regularly. Therefore, lifestyle differences conservatively represent 5,000 calories, or about 1½ pounds of body fat per week. Do you still wonder why people are overweight and why weight seems to steadily creep higher?

Chapter 2

PROTEIN

THE BODY USES PROTEIN TO BUILD TISSUE FOR GROWTH AND REPAIR. Protein is not a single substance; chains of chemicals called amino acids make up protein. Different proteins have different combinations and amounts of amino acids in them. Our bodies contain hundreds of different proteins, each with special properties and functions, yet we can manufacture only 13 amino acids. Our diets must contain a variety of protein sources to obtain the other nine amino acids, which are called essential amino acids.

Complete protein foods are those supplying sufficient amounts of all nine essential amino acids. Such food comes from animal sources. Plant proteins lack at least one of the nine essential amino acids and are therefore called incomplete proteins. However, as I will explain, by combining a plant protein with a grain, a complete protein is formed.

The amino acids combine with other substances in the body and link to build tissue. If, due to an unbalanced diet, one amino acid is in short supply or not available, the others cannot be used to form a complete protein. On the other hand, consuming too much of certain amino acids can interfere with the metabolizing of others. For this reason protein supplements (which supply too much of some amino acids) can be harmful.

THINK TWICE ABOUT ANIMAL PROTEIN

The problem with foods we typically think of as high in protein is that protein is not always the main ingredient. Compared to some plant proteins, meat is protein rich and contains all nine essential amino acids. However, most cuts of meat are also high in fat and provide more calories from fat than from protein. To make matters worse, half the fat in meat is usually saturated. A T-bone steak provides only 20% of its calories from protein; the remaining calories are from fat. A well-trimmed T-bone is a 50/50 split between fat and protein. Since we typically eat far more meat than we need to provide our daily protein requirement, we eat too much protein.

Such a diet also dangerously increases our consumption of saturated fat.

Dairy proteins can also be high in fat. Hard cheeses like Cheddar are 25% protein and 75% fat. Two percent milk does not contain 2% of its calories as fat; 37% of the calories are fat. Most fish is low in fat, if simply cooked. But canned tuna packed in oil is 34% protein and 64% fat; draining the oil changes the ratio to 58% protein and 37% calories from fat. I will show you how to reduce your consumption of high-fat animal protein, but first there are a couple of other meat-related issues to address.

IS YOUR MEAT SAFE TO EAT?

One health problem is the contamination of meat and poultry that is processed for mass market consumption. Many animals frequently receive a variety of hormones and antibiotics, which accumulate in their flesh. Large processing plants often do not observe required standards of hygiene. Meat can be contaminated with feces, urine, bone and teeth fragments. Some of this contamination regularly causes illness and even death. Luncheon meats, sausages and hot dogs often contain substandard animal parts. Eating animal hooves, bones and unmentionable parts won't make you ill, but I don't consider it appealing, either.

In the name of safety, government regulators tell us to respect expiry dates on packages; to cook meat until the internal temperature is 165°F; to not let juices from raw meat contact other food; and to clean our hands, cutting boards and all utensils thoroughly after handling meat. To my way of thinking, why take the health risks associated with eating possibly tainted low-quality products? Buy high-quality meat and fowl from a reputable source that checks its processors. Or eat less meat so you can afford the good stuff.

HOW TO REDUCE YOUR MEAT CONSUMPTION

If you want to eat less meat, try spaghetti sauce with a small amount of meat in it, or eat half to a third of a steak and make vegetables or pasta the main course. You can also choose meat that is lower in fat. Fish (except salmon, trout, turbot and sardines) is a lean source of protein. And ounce for ounce, white chicken meat provides more protein than steak — and half the fat. Macaroni with low-fat cheese is an excellent non-meat source of protein and provides carbohydrates as well. Cereal with milk is another great protein/carbohydrate combination.

Consider that for a 120-pound person the Recommended Daily Allowance — RDA — for protein is 44 grams, and for a 150-pound person 55 grams. (Pregnant and lactating women need an extra 20 to 25 grams of protein daily). Each ounce of animal protein — most meat, chicken and fish — provides 7 grams of protein. By eating only 4 to 6 ounces of animal protein per day *in a balanced diet*, you will consume an adequate amount of *total protein*.

If you consume plant sources to meet more of your protein needs, you are eating protein and carbohydrate instead of protein and fat. The richest sources of vegetable protein are legumes — dried split peas and beans. Kidney beans, for example, provide 25% of their calories from protein and 70% from carbohydrate. A half cup of cooked kidney beans or lentils has 7 to 8 grams of protein, essential minerals, only 107 calories and virtually no fat. And a half cup of cooked soybeans packs 10 grams of protein. These are the cheapest source of protein, gram for gram.

EXAMPLES OF HIGH-PROTEIN FOODS OTHER THAN MEAT

Food	Portion	Protein (g)
soybeans	1 cup	20.0
lentils	1 cup	15.5
cottage cheese	⅔ cup	14.0
tofu	4 oz	up to 14.0
split-pea soup	¾ cup cooked peas	12.0
milk (skim)	1 cup	8.0
Cheddar cheese	1 oz	7.0
egg	1 large	6.5

COMPLETE PROTEINS

Animal proteins and one source of plant protein — soybeans or tofu — are the only protein sources that supply sufficient amounts of all nine essential amino acids, and are therefore complete proteins. Additionally, textured vegetable protein (TVP), which is made from soybeans, is a complete source of protein. However, with very little effort you can create complete proteins without eating animal flesh or tofu. Eating a combination of legumes with grains provides all the essential amino acids that make up a complete protein. And plant protein is not of inferior quality to animal protein.

It used to be thought that incomplete proteins should be combined in the same meal, a technique called protein complementing, and popular articles on vegetarianism still push this practice. Recent research, however, concludes that by consuming different proteins on the same day your requirements for complete protein will be met.

Legume or plant protein sources include any dried beans or peas such as black beans, kidney beans, navy beans, pinto beans, soybeans, black-eyed peas, chick peas, split peas and lentils. It does not make a difference, from a health point of view, whether these plant proteins are canned or dried. The advantage to cans is that you don't have to soak beans and peas overnight in water before cooking them.

To ensure that you consume all essential amino acids on a given day, one or more plant sources must be combined with a grain, such as barley, bulgur, corn, couscous, kasha, millet, oats, quinoa (pronounced "keen-wha," and the highest protein source of any grain), millet, rice or wheat. Seeds and nuts can be combined with grains to form a complete protein, but these are high in fat, and should be eaten in moderation.

Finally, note that eggs and dairy products, because they come from animal sources, are complete proteins, so lacto-ovo vegetarians (those who also consume milk, cheese and eggs) need not worry about complementing protein.

MODERATE PROTEIN CONSUMPTION IS THE KEY

Because the body's capacity to store protein is limited, protein must be consumed daily, although a few days without will not harm a healthy person. If you don't eat enough protein, your body searches out the most readily available source of protein, which is your own lean muscle tissue. Your body will begin to draw on the protein in muscles to provide protein for vital organs. However, the error that most North Americans make is not eating too little protein, it's eating too much protein. Remember, we should consume 55% of our calories from carbohydrates, 15% from protein and no more than 30% from fat.

Eating a high-protein diet without carbohydrates leads to excessive fluid loss. The digestion of protein requires a lot of water. For this reason high-protein diets are dehydrating. On such diets you lose weight rapidly because you are losing water, not fat! After you follow a high-protein diet for even a short time, consuming a carbohydrate, such as bread, will cause your body to reabsorb fluid. A couple of pieces of bread act like a sponge, helping to absorb as much as four pounds of water. You swell up like a balloon!

Aside from pregnancy and lactation, the only times your body's protein requirement increases is following illness, such as flu, fever or diarrhea, and after injury, surgery or severe emotional stress. Consume 20 to 45% over the RDA (depending on the severity of your illness or stress) during your recovery period.

Unless you are subject to extreme physical demands, if you eat a balanced diet you will get plenty of protein. Even strict vegan vegetarians will not have a problem if they eat the proper combinations of grains and legumes. And athletes get enough protein because they eat more food. If, for example, body builders consume 3,500 calories a day and 15% of these come from protein, they are consuming more than 130 grams of protein — perhaps even too much. Many people should be more concerned with getting enough complex carbohydrates and keeping fat intake to acceptable levels.

PROTEIN SUPPLEMENTS

Let's clear up some other protein myths, as well. Healthy individuals don't digest "hydrolyzed" protein (that which has been broken down into amino acids) any better than whole protein. In spite of claims for the wonders of hydrolyzed proteins and other amino acid supplements, taking too much of one amino acid may interfere with the absorption of others. In the end, protein synthesis can be inhibited and a variety of health problems may result.

Much of the information about the benefits of high-tech protein powders, liquids or tablets and amino acid supplements is manufacturers' hype. I have even seen articles in well-respected body building magazines, written by authors with Ph.D.'s, that are disappointingly unscientific and very misleading. Controlled studies involving athletes have not supported the claims made for supplements. Furthermore, athletes who attribute benefits to such supplements may not have been eating properly to begin with, or perhaps lucrative endorsement contracts somewhat swayed their opinion.

MILK

Milk is a good source of high-quality protein that contains more carbohydrates — 12 grams per cup — than either protein or fat. Unfortunately, milk's main carbohydrate — the sugar lactose — is not easily digestible by many people. About two-thirds of the world's population begin to become lactose intolerant around the age of two. When such people consume more than a certain amount of milk or milk products they may suffer from gas, bloating, abdominal cramps and diarrhea.

The intestinal enzyme lactase allows milk to be broken down and digested. Lactase levels decrease after the first year or two of life. To compensate, either Lactaid milk can be used, or Lact-Aid, an artificial lactase replacement, can be added to dairy products. However, most people will find that drinking moderate amounts of milk produces no symptoms, especially when the milk is consumed slowly along with other foods. Some milk products, such as yogurt, non-processed cheese and buttermilk, have acceptably reduced lactose levels.

Chapter 3
CARBOHYDRATES

ABOUT 10 YEARS AGO HIGH-PROTEIN DIETS WERE THE RAGE. WE NOW have a better understanding of what's good for us. We've learned, for example, that meats are high in fat and that carbohydrates are low in fat and are the body's largest energy source. Conveniently, natural, unprocessed carbohydrates are rich in vital nutrients, often contain protein and are the only foods not linked to any major disease. In fact, numerous studies have confirmed that a high-carbohydrate, low-fat diet can reduce the risk of five of the 10 leading causes of death in North America: coronary heart disease, stroke, arteriosclerosis (hardening of the arteries), diabetes and some cancers.

Rather than focusing on carbohydrates, many people who still have a high-protein mindset fool themselves into thinking that hot dogs and luncheon meat are the only cuts of meat they can afford. Cheap meats are actually expensive sources of protein, as they are mostly fat. It's better to eat 2 or 3 ounces of good-quality meat less often and to eat more complex carbohydrates.

The term "complex carbohydrates" refers to a huge variety of foods — fruits, vegetables, legumes and grains; in fact, all sugars and starches and most fibres that we eat. The common element among these foods is that the body transforms the carbohydrates in them into its basic fuel, glucose. Small amounts of glucose can be stored by our liver and muscles as glycogen and can be quickly transformed back into glucose for release into the bloodstream to meet our energy demands.

The body's general ability to store carbohydrates is limited. So we should eat a high-*carbohydrate* diet. We should not, however, eat a high-*calorie* diet to get the carbohydrates that we need. Excess carbohydrates, amounts above those that can be stored, are converted into fat and then stored. To strike a balance, we should consume 55% of our daily caloric intake from complex carbohydrates. And we should limit simple carbohydrates to 15% of our consumption.

In contrast to complex carbohydrates, simple carbohydrates are sugars like glucose, fructose and other "oses." Simple carbohydrate foods are "empty calorie" foods because few nutrients accompany the sugar. You eat a lot of calories, but you don't feel full. A simple carbohydrate, like a chocolate bar, can have 300 calories, the same number of calories as in the following complex carbohydrate foods: four small apples or bananas, two medium baked potatoes, or a huge salad with low-cal dressing. What would fill you up more?

A terrific benefit of foods high in complex carbohydrates is that they contain lots of water or fibre or both. If you are watching your weight, you will find them low in calories but filling, allowing you to vary your diet in a satisfying and effective way. Be aware, however: a diet rich in carbohydrates and deficient in protein will lead to fluid retention and an uncomfortable bloated feeling. Balancing these food sources minimizes weight fluctuations and ensures that you feel healthy and energetic.

I strongly recommend *unrefined* carbohydrates to my clients because carbohydrates lose nutrients when they are processed. For example, unrefined flour has about 75% more essential nutrients than refined flour. Enriched (refined) flour has most of its B vitamins replaced, but none of the fibre that was lost during processing. *Whole grain* breads provide the most nutrients, and 100% whole wheat is the next best choice.

Because three-quarters of us still prefer soft white bread, manufacturers offer us "brown" bread, or a variety of "whole wheat" breads, which are really just refined white flour with little or no whole grain but with some colouring added for effect. This lets us eat mushy white bread and think it's healthy. We can't entirely blame the baker for this ploy. As we change our attitudes, food producers are quick to respond.

As with bread, enriched or whole grain noodles are the best pasta choices. However, "instant" or "minute" rices are refined like white bread. If you don't have time to cook brown rice at dinner time, make it ahead and freeze it in individual or family-size portions. It's higher in fibre and minerals than white rice. (There is no difference, nutritionally, between long- and short-grain rice.)

CARBOHYDRATE LOADING

Fit people can store greater amounts of carbohydrate as glycogen than non-fit people. Depleted glycogen stores may be the reason some people find that regular exercise, instead of providing energy for work and play, leaves them feeling dragged out. For the two hours immediately after prolonged exercise our muscles can store carbohydrates at a greatly accelerated rate. So eat a high-carbohydrate post-exercise meal.

Athletes take note, if you are not yet aware, there has been considerable modification to the classic "carbo-loading" routine, which tended to produce several undesirable side effects, including weight gain, lethargy and abnormal heart beat. Generally, the best way to carbo-load is to increase your complex carbohydrate consumption and decrease your level of exercise during the three days before an endurance event. Although each coach will have exact formulas by which to do so, remember that we can store only so much carbohydrate as glycogen; the rest turns to fat.

Chapter 4

FIBRE

ALTHOUGH INTEREST IN HIGH-FIBRE FOODS DATES BACK TO THE ANCIENT
Greeks, the benefits of fibre have become much better known
during the past 20 or so years. During our childhoods, many of
us were introduced to fibre as "roughage" or "bulk" foods. We
were told to fill up on them so that we would not have as much
room for fattening foods. That was good advice, but recent research
has added a lot more good news to the story.

Studies reveal that in nations where people eat high-fibre foods,
there are significantly fewer cases of colon and rectal cancers,
diverticulosis, haemorrhoids, heart disease and other ailments.
Fibre also appears to play a large role in reducing the risk of other
chronic disorders, such as diabetes. And it plays a major role in
preventing digestive disorders, some of which are very uncomfortable even in a mild form. Most foods that are high in fibre are
also full of carbohydrates, vitamins and minerals, and low in fat.
Increased fibre consumption leads to a healthier diet.

Fibre is a large group of different substances that have several
effects on the body. All fibres come from plant sources. There are
two broad categories of fibre — soluble and insoluble — although
most foods contain both types. Soluble fibre dissolves easily in
water and is digestible. Oat bran, the subject of much hype a few
years ago, is an example. Insoluble fibre cannot be digested and
is good for bowel regularity. Wheat bran is an example.

SOLUBLE FIBRE

- Soluble fibre prevents or slows the absorption of certain substances
  into the bloodstream. For example, it slows the entry of glucose
  into the blood, producing a more even rise in blood sugar. This
  characteristic makes it especially important to people with diabetes and to those who eat a lot of sugary snack foods.
- Soluble fibre is thought to lower blood cholesterol by slowing
  the liver's production of cholesterol and/or by forming a gel
  around cholesterol in the blood so it can be carried out of the

bloodstream. It is found in apples, barley, beans, bran, brown rice, oats, oat bran, lentils and Metamucil.

INSOLUBLE FIBRE

- Because it is not digested, insoluble fibre serves important functions and plays a significant role in disease prevention. As it passes through the intestinal tract it absorbs excess water and swells. This makes stools less packed and easier to pass. Insoluble fibre is particularly helpful when you are constipated.
- Indigestible fibre speeds the passage of food through the colon. The faster passage reduces the amount of time that any metabolic waste or carcinogen present in food will be in contact with the colon walls. Therefore, such fibre is associated with lowered risk of colon cancer and diverticulosis.
- It is found in wheat bran and other whole grains, prunes, beans, lentils and the skins of fruits and vegetables. Processing — milling, peeling and extracting — removes the fibrous outer material. Unprocessed foods retain fibre and are better for us.

FIBRE-RELATED DISORDERS

Constipation is the inability to have a bowel movement after three or more days. Drinking adequate amounts of fluid, getting regular exercise and eating a diet containing lots of fibre usually solve this problem. Insoluble fibre, when consumed with sufficient fluid, increases the frequency and ease of bowel movements by absorbing water to produce a softer, less packed stool that can pass more quickly through the intestines. (Avoid laxatives, if possible. They have side effects, such as bloating, gas, diarrhea and abdominal cramping. You also can become dependent on them for normal bowel movements. No one should use laxatives regularly without first consulting a doctor, and laxatives should not be used as a substitute for a proper diet and a healthy, active lifestyle.)

Frequently, when beginning a weight-loss program, people find they are constipated. As they consume less fat, which lubricates the bowel, and more fibre, to which the digestive system must adjust, some constipation is not abnormal. Unless you feel uncomfortable, a bowel movement every two to three days is common when you restrict caloric intake.

Don't eat too much cheese, which is constipating, as is medication containing codeine. Finally, constipation is common during the premenstrual period. (See question 22 on page 133 for the role of nutrition in relieving menstrual discomfort.)

Diverticulitis is a condition in which tiny pouches that trap food form in the wall of the colon. These pouches can become painfully inflamed. If they burst, the situation is serious. The condition is common in people over 40 and very common in those over 50, although I've seen it occur in harried businesspeople in their early 30s! Eating insoluble fibre seems to prevent this condition.

Cancer of the colon is the second most common form of cancer in North America. It is rare in people who eat a diet of high-fibre foods and little red meat. Insoluble fibre may inhibit the development of precancerous colon and rectal polyps and shrink developing polyps. In various studies, fibre was shown to be helpful for both high-risk groups and the population at large. Given the prevalence of this deadly cancer, the objection to regular rectal examinations is a form of Russian roulette. (In those over 50, or in cases of a strong family history of cancer in individuals over 40, rectal exams should be part of a yearly medical checkup.) Opposition from insurance companies is strictly from a cost containment viewpoint and not based on health considerations.

Although findings are not yet complete, a link between *breast cancer* and a low-fibre diet is also being explored. However, women who consume high-fibre diets typically eat less fat. As fat consumption may play a role in breast cancer, cancer specialists suggest a low-fat, high-fibre diet for women of all ages. Fibrous foods are usually high in antioxidants like beta carotene and vitamin C, which may help protect us against a variety of cancers.

Heart Disease. The effect of oat bran on heart disease has received the most press, but other sources of soluble fibre also appear to have a moderately positive effect. Soluble fibre helps reduce total cholesterol, possibly through a reduction of LDL, the bad cholesterol. And a high-fibre, low-fat diet also contributes to the beneficial effect that fibre alone has on cholesterol.

Diabetes responds well to a high-carbohydrate, high-fibre diet. Research has shown that diabetics can substantially reduce their insulin requirements and improve glucose tolerance by altering their diets. This change requires strict supervision by a doctor.

Gallstones do not seem to form as frequently in those who eat a high-fibre diet.

Obesity and low-fibre diets go hand in hand. Fibrous foods, filling and low in fat, are great for weight control. Beware of fibre supplements — pills — to help lose weight. There is not yet conclusive evidence that they are effective. And such synthetic sources of fibre are not as effective as natural ones; they don't provide vitamins and minerals; they are expensive, as high doses are required; and they frequently require adherence to some gimmick diet. Read the label before buying fibre bars, often high in sugar and fat.

INCREASING YOUR FIBRE CONSUMPTION

It's easy to increase daily intake of dietary fibre, but do so gradually to prevent gas or cramps. Current recommendations suggest we eat 30 grams of fibre daily as a safe and healthy level. Most vegetarians eat 40 to 50 grams. The average North American, who eats refined flour and sugary processed foods, consumes only 12 to 15 grams. By eating ½ cup of All-Bran (which tastes great), Bran Buds or 100% Bran cereal, you get 10 grams of fibre. The following guidelines will help you consume adequate fibre:

- Eat a variety of unprocessed foods including grains, legumes, lentils, beans and brown rice. If beans cause flatulence, try adding a few drops of Beano to your meal. It is available in pharmacies and health food stores and seems to work miracles.
- Fruits and vegetables are a good source of fibre. Many fruits and vegetables, if properly washed, can be eaten unpeeled — the skins are high in fibre and vitamins. Fruit juices have no fibre and raise your blood sugar rapidly, but raw fruit is a source of fibre and doesn't affect blood sugar adversely.
- Drink adequate liquid — 6 to 8 glasses — during the day so the fibre will help your digestion.
- Spread your intake of fibre over the course of the day to eliminate gas or bloating. And don't increase fibre consumption too quickly. Over a week or two work up to the equivalent of ½ to 1 cup of All-Bran per day.
- Don't just sprinkle bran on everything that you eat. Eat a vari-

ety of fibrous foods. Prunes, raisins and figs are particularly potent dietary remedies for constipation — but don't overdo it. Moderation and a consistent variety of foods are essential to regularity. Most doctors now recognize fibre as the first line of defence against constipation. Although some people may need to use laxatives, you will be surprised how much of a difference dietary change will make.

The following list shows the amount of fibre in common foods. However, there is not yet one accepted way to measure total (soluble and insoluble) fibre, so values will vary from list to list. Nearly all fruits, vegetables and whole grain products contain some of both types of fibre.

APPROXIMATE FIBRE CONTENT OF COMMON FOODS

Food	Portion	Fibre(g)
white bread	1 slice	0.6
cracked wheat bread	1 slice	1.4
whole wheat bread	1 slice	1.8
Bran Flakes	½ cup	3.7
Corn Flakes	½ cup	1.6
high fibre cereal (All-Bran, Bran Buds or 100% Bran)	½ cup	10.1
oat bran, cooked	½ cup	7.5
oatmeal	½ cup	1.1
Rice Krispies	½ cup	0.7
Shredded Wheat	1 biscuit	3.1
apple (with skin)	½	1.5
apricot	1	0.5
banana	½	0.9 – 2.5
blueberries	½ cup	1.7
cantaloupe	¼ medium	2.0

grapefruit	½ medium	1.1
nectarine	1	2.2
orange	1	3.0
peach	1	2.3
pear	½ large	3.1
plum	1 large	0.8
prunes, stewed	½ cup	8.3
raspberries	½ cup	3.1
strawberries	¾ cup	2.4
asparagus	6 medium stalks	3.6
broccoli	1 cup	6.4
Brussels sprouts	1 cup	4.4
cabbage, cooked	1 cup	4.1
corn	1 cup	3.0
carrots	1 large / 3 small	5.7
cauliflower, cooked	1 cup	2.3
green pepper, cooked	1 cup	1.5
lettuce	1 cup	0.8
potato	1	3.9
tomato, canned	1 cup	2.0
baked beans, canned	½ cup	5.5
kidney beans	½ cup cooked	6.9
lentils	½ cup cooked	5.2
peas, canned	½ cup	6.0
brown rice	½ cup cooked	2.4
white rice	½ cup cooked	0.8
pasta	½ cup cooked	1.0

Chapter 5
SODIUM

ASIDE FROM SUGAR, SODIUM OR TABLE SALT IS THE MOST COMMONLY used food additive. You may have read reports indicating that lack of calcium, rather than excess salt consumption, is tied more closely to blood pressure problems. But salt does play a significant role in sensitive individuals.

Not everyone with high blood pressure is sensitive to salt. And of course not everyone who eats too much salt will develop high blood pressure. But in countries where salt consumption is excessive, high blood pressure is common. It seems that about 15 to 20% of us are prone to developing high blood pressure and therefore must control our salt intake.

The problem is that high-risk individuals have no way of telling who they are before high blood pressure develops. And once you have symptoms of high blood pressure, serious damage may have already occurred. If you have a family history of hypertension (high blood pressure), strictly limit your salt consumption and have regular checkups. And because all of us are at risk to a variety of modern-day afflictions, we should all consider a balanced lifestyle and a regular medical exam as our first line of defence. It is also prudent for all of us to moderate our consumption of salt.

Our bodies need sodium to conduct nerve signals; to allow muscles to contract; and to maintain fluid balance. But too much can cause water retention, which makes us feel bloated and heavy; it aggravates PMS symptoms; and it impairs athletic performance.

There is enough sodium naturally present in food and water to meet the needs of the average person, but this does not stop us from craving more. Manufacturers capitalize on our tastes by heavily salting most convenience foods to add flavour. When used in cooking or processing, as opposed to being sprinkled on at the table, a lot more is required to enhance flavour. As a result, about two-thirds of the salt that we eat comes from processed or convenience foods.

At least 70 compounds used to make food contain sodium. Even foods we don't consider high in salt frequently are. So going wild on the obviously salty choices like Chinese food, chips, pickles and so forth is a real gamble. Unless you perspire profusely on your job, you generally should limit your consumption to about 2,000 mg of sodium daily — the equivalent of one teaspoon. Most of us far exceed this amount; we consume 5,000 to 7,000 mg per day without realizing it. Let's deal with some excessive sources of salt.

Most of us know that Chinese food is high in salt. But the two ingredients that contribute to its sodium content are present in more than Chinese food alone. Soy sauce, while having only 15 calories per tablespoon, has a whopping 1,000 mg of sodium — and who uses just one tablespoon? If you cook with soy sauce at home, try sodium-reduced brands, which have half the normal sodium. Be sure to refrigerate them after opening because sodium, which acts as a preservative, is not present in sufficient quantity to do so. Chinese food, and many prepared foods such as flavoured rice and frozen meals, frequently contain monosodium glutamate, or MSG, as a flavour enhancer. MSG is another form of salt. Always read package labels.

Generally, the more processed the food the higher its salt content. For example, a fresh tomato has only 5 mg of sodium. Tomato juice has 500 mg or more per cup, and a cup of canned tomato soup has about 1,100 mg. Prepared frozen pancakes contain between 400 mg and 800 mg for a serving of three, and a slice of pizza has anywhere from 500 to 1,000 mg. A complete frozen dinner can pack 2,000 mg!

Become aware of some of the less-known sources of salt. Two slices of processed white bread can contain 230 mg, one serving of instant pudding or pie filling can have 400 mg, and one ounce of cold cereal can have 250 mg. Proteins also can be high in sodium content. A can of tuna contains up to 500 mg. Cottage cheese has 440 mg per half cup, low-fat hard cheese has up to 600 mg per 1.5 ounces, and of course smoked meats, ham and smoked fish are all culprits. One small hot dog has 550 mg, and fast-food hamburgers have 500 mg (quarter-pounders have 1,000 mg). Even club soda is high in sodium, as it is carbonated with sodium compounds. Popcorn, especially that served at the movies, can have

300 mg of salt added to each one cup serving — 2,700 mg per small bag — enough to make the average dieter swell like a balloon!

There, I think I've mentioned just about everything you love to eat regularly. Don't worry: you don't have to avoid these foods. Just consider your daily sodium intake when planning meals and snacks. And there are solutions. Here are some suggestions:

- Drain and rinse canned foods to remove the brine, which is where most of the salt is.
- Buy more fresh food. If you don't already do so, try a bit of cooking. Several of my recipes are simple to make and freeze well. Prepare them in quantity on a weekend.
- Meat, chicken and fish you cook yourself should not be salted before cooking. Add a little salt afterward if you need to. You'll use much less this way.
- The water used to cook pasta and vegetables does not have to be salted.
- Some recipes for soups and sauces call for salt, or for flavourings such as soy sauce that are high in sodium. Try using half of the suggested amount to begin with and then taste. Frequently a bit of salt sprinkled on a dish at the table goes a lot farther than salt used in the cooking.
- Experiment using less salt when cooking stews and similar dishes. If you use bouillon cubes to make stock, use low-sodium cubes.
- Read labels. Additives containing the word "sodium" are all sources of salt, such as sodium benzoate, sodium propionate and sodium bicarbonate (baking soda). Baking powder also contains some salt.
- Most processed foods and many prepared foods now also come in low-sodium varieties. Although such foods often taste different from the regular choices, you can add herbs and spices such as garlic or onion powder (not garlic salt or onion salt), sweet or hot peppers, flavoured vinegars and pepper, lemon or lime, dried mustard, oregano, curry and so on. You will be pleasantly surprised.
- Check the labels of prepared entrees and meals for their sodium content. Some varieties are better than others.

- Try salt-free popcorn. I make it in the microwave and I like it better now. Try fat-free, salt-free tacos, such as Guiltless Gourmet, and dip them in salsa.
- Many of us salt our food as a habit, without even tasting it first. If you were to eat food with little or no salt for a few days and then return to your usual amount of salting, you probably would no longer enjoy the food. It's amazing how sensitive your taste buds can become to a flavour when given some variety. Constant exposure to the same flavours dulls our taste buds.
- Naturally carbonated mineral waters are much lower in sodium than club soda. Cott, Reinhart, Canada Dry and President's Choice all make salt-free club soda.
- Tap water can be high in sodium. Where water is "soft," it is sodium that softens it. Although health officials recommend no more than 45 parts per million (ppm) of sodium per 8 ounces of tap water, in some areas of North America levels can reach 400 ppm. Even 100 ppm can contribute to elevated blood pressure. If you live in a city, call your municipal water works to find out the sodium level in your water supply.
- Sodium is common in some medical remedies such as antacids. Alka-Seltzer contains 500 mg per dose and Bromo-Seltzer has 700 mg. For alternative tips on dealing with acid indigestion see the answer to question 20 (page 132).
- I don't recommend salt substitutes unless you take them under the supervision of your doctor. These contain potassium chloride instead of sodium chloride, and an overdose can be dangerous. Mrs. Dash, Spike or President's Choice Too Good To Be True Lemon Herb Seasoning are better alternatives.

Salt causes the kidneys to absorb fluid into the body, so an average person can gain up to five pounds after a salty meal like Chinese food or cold cuts. If you are trying to lose weight and eating high-sodium foods, your weight loss is bound to slow down. Similarly, if weight loss suddenly plateaus, or your weight increases quickly, review your sodium intake and try to adjust it accordingly.

When on a calorie-restricted diet, some people may eat too little salt. When we're trying to lose weight, we eat less food than usual, and we may therefore consume less salt than we normally would. Reduced salt consumption decreases fluid retention, which leads to lower blood volume. This is not dangerous unless we are dehydrating ourselves, but lower blood volume will reduce our blood pressure.

Obviously, for many of us, lower blood pressure is a good thing. However, people who have low blood pressure to begin with might feel light-headed, dizzy or headachy when restricting their food consumption. The easiest way to determine if your blood pressure is at fault is to have it tested. If your blood pressure is low, eating a bit more salt is acceptable. Any symptoms should disappear within 20 minutes of ingesting a salty food.

If this doesn't work, try eating an orange or half a banana. Occasionally, when losing weight and eating less salt, potassium also will be flushed from the system, as it, too, is water soluble. These fruits will replace the lost potassium.

Finally, after intense exercise or a bout of diarrhea or vomiting, loss of fluid and sodium may make us crave salt. This is a normal reaction to salt deficiency. But a need for sodium is not the reason for the daily salt cravings people often experience. Such cravings develop with increasing exposure to salty food. Think of all of the times you may have experienced such feelings and not known why — another reason to avoid junk food.

Chapter 6
SUGAR

ALL JOKES ASIDE, WOLFING DOWN A DOUGHNUT OR CHOCOLATE BAR does not qualify as carbohydrate loading. *Complex* carbohydrates include grains, rice, pasta, fruits and vegetables. Simple carbohydrates are all sugar, and include table sugar, honey, jam, candies and sweetened beverages. The average North American eats about 400 to 500 calories of such sweetening each day, far more than our ancestors consumed.

Complex carbohydrates are full of fibre, and the glucose in them is absorbed slowly into the bloodstream. Their consumption leads to a gentle increase in blood sugar and a slow, sustainable rise in energy levels. Most sweetened snack foods, on the other hand, have no nutritional value. They do not contain any fibre, and are absorbed rapidly into the blood. This leads to a rapid rise in blood sugar levels and an energy lift that lasts about 20 minutes. When the fuel runs out, the symptoms are not pleasant.

Here's how it works. The body's normal response to an elevated sugar level is to lower the sugar level through the release of insulin by the pancreas. The insulin helps to transport the sugar from your blood to the cells, where it is used as fuel. When some people eat a pure sugary food, too much sugar is cleared from the blood. The result is a blood sugar "crash." This happens especially when they eat a sugary food on an empty stomach.

Even when something like a chocolate bar is consumed after a meal, 30 or 40 minutes later one's blood sugar level may be too low for proper functioning. They may become faint, shaky, irritable or nauseated — all symptoms often confused with stress and anxiety. They also may crave more sugar to raise their blood sugar back to normal.

In moderation and when not used as an alternative to real food, sugar will not cause a blood sugar crash, nor is it harmful to the average person. But it is not nutritious, either. Because it supplies calories and nothing else — no fibre, vitamins or minerals — it's referred to as an "empty calorie" food.

I'll bet you're thinking about honey and brown sugar. Aren't they more nutritious than white sugar? Sorry, this is another myth. Even honey straight from the hive has insignificant food value, and brown sugar is merely white sugar with a little molasses added for colouring. And Demerara, while less refined, is no more nutritious than other sugars. As for calories, white sugar has 46 to 52 per tablespoon, brown sugar has about 52, and honey has 60 to 64.

Ketchup, crackers, bread, canned soup, cereals, peanut butter, salad dressing and spaghetti sauce may contain sugar — another reason to read labels. By the way, granola is high not only in sugar but in fat, too.

Next myth — that foods that are labelled "sugar-free" are low in calories. Unfortunately, "sugar-free" foods, such as those for diabetics, are frequently higher in calories than the original because the manufacturer has replaced the sugar with fat, and fats have nine calories per gram. All carbohydrates, including sugar, have only four calories per gram. Another problem is that "sugar-free" by definition means "sucrose-free." However, this does not rule out other forms of sweetening such as honey or corn syrup. Always read the label. To find alternatives to sugary snacks, see the answer to question 18 on page 130, and try my recipes that use Splenda brand sweetener.

When you have a cold or sore throat, look for sugar-free products. Neo-Citran's sugar-free drink has about 35 calories. Cepastat is a strong sugar-free throat lozenge and is available at most pharmacy counters. Soothease is also sugar-free, but not as strong; it's available at candy counters. Benelyn makes a good sugar-free cough syrup.

SUGAR CONTENT OF POPULAR FOODS

Food	Portion	Sugar (teaspoons)
Chocolate bar	1 oz	7
Iced chocolate cake	1 slice	15
Ice cream	½ cup	5
Sherbet	½ cup	7

Apple pie	1 slice	12
Coke	12 oz	8
Orange juice	8 oz	7
Ketchup	1 tablespoon	1
Cereal	½ cup	0–5 (read label)

Chapter 7
CAFFEINE AND ALCOHOL

THERE'S NOTHING LIKE A CUP OF GOOD COFFEE FIRST THING IN THE morning. Great taste, warming in winter, the perfect breakfast substitute — or so it seems. The real reason we go for that early-morning cup is that our blood sugar is low when we get up, as we haven't eaten for about 10 hours. Since our stomachs are empty, the caffeine is immediately absorbed into our bloodstream (much faster than food) and causes blood sugar levels to rise. That's the good news; the rest is bad news.

To lower blood sugar, an insulin secretion follows. The problem is that some people secrete excess insulin, causing blood sugar to drop to the previously low level or to a level lower than before that first cup of coffee. They frequently feel worse than if they had no caffeine at all. The typical response is to have a second cup of coffee, and the process begins again. The more caffeine we drink, the greater the likelihood of this overcompensating blood sugar response.

Caffeine is not terrible and does not have to be avoided altogether. The problems arise when we use it, instead of food, for energy, because it then wreaks havoc on our metabolism and the way we feel. We get energy through the day from short bursts of caffeine and then wonder why we always feel lousy, or why we can't concentrate without another cup of coffee. Also remember that too much caffeine can cause jitters, anxiety and insomnia. Even moderate consumption can trigger an anxiety attack in some individuals.

These are not the only side effects caused by this drug. Caffeine is a natural diuretic, causing water to be excreted in our urine. Along with the water, we lose water-soluble vitamins such as B and C, and minerals such as calcium. Vitamin deficiencies lead to all sorts of problems for all of us, but calcium deficiency is a major problem for women over 40. Lack of calcium contributes to osteoporosis — weak and brittle bones.

There are naturally occurring compounds, called tannins, in both caffeinated and decaffeinated coffee and tea. They reduce the absorption of nutrients from the food we eat immediately before or while we have these drinks. Iron absorption, for example, can be reduced by up to half. For women with an iron deficiency, excess consumption of these beverages can be a serious matter. You may want to reconsider having such drinks with or immediately after your meals.

Caffeine also increases the secretion of acids in our stomachs, contributing to acid indigestion or heart burn and aggravating ulcers and hiatus hernias. In fact, both caffeinated and decaf coffee are major contributors to heart burn — particularly if they are consumed on an empty stomach.

As if these complications weren't enough, here's the biggy: insulin is known as a fat-hoarding hormone because it inhibits fat mobilization from our cells. Because caffeine causes the release of insulin, excess consumption makes it more difficult to lose weight. Finally, note that caffeine readily crosses the placenta, so it can affect the fetus. Frequently women don't know they're pregnant for the first six weeks. So if you are even trying to become pregnant, you should avoid caffeine.

Consumed in moderation, coffee and tea can be enjoyable and probably won't produce any symptoms. I tell my clients to listen to their bodies when it comes to the effects of coffee and tea and to try decaffeinated beverages, herbal teas and coffee substitutes. Finally, if you're a heavy user and decide to cut back, take note that you are reducing your consumption of a serious drug. You may experience withdrawal headaches for seven to ten days. Cut back gradually, by one cup per day, to minimize symptoms. And ride it out. The long-term benefits are worth it.

COUNTING CAFFEINE

	Portion	Caffeine (mg)
Coffee, drip	6–8 oz	110–150
Coffee, perk	6–8 oz	60–125
Coffee, instant	6–8 oz	40–105
Espresso & cappuccino	4–6 oz	varies tremendously

Coffee, decaf.	6–8 oz	2–5
Tea, 5-minute steep	6–8 oz	40–100
Tea, 3 minute steep	6–8 oz	20–50
Hot chocolate	6–8 oz	2–10
Cola*	12 oz	30–45
Milk chocolate	1 oz	1–15
Bittersweet chocolate	1 oz	5–35
Chocolate cake	1 slice	20–30

*A young child gets the same caffeine kick from a can of pop that an adult gets from 3 or 4 cups of coffee.

THE FRENCH PARODOX

In Chapter 1, I discussed the role of alcohol in slowing fat metabolism, and in Chapter 12, tricks to reduce alcohol consumption on social occasions. Please don't think I'm against drinking. In fact, it would be irresponsible not to acknowledge evidence that links moderate (one to two drinks a day) consumption of alcohol to increased HDL cholesterol levels and a lower risk of heart disease. This connection between alcohol and a healthy heart was publicized in media accounts of French eating and drinking habits: daily drinkers had a lower incidence of heart disease than abstainers, regardless of their typically high fat intake. This relationship has been called the French Paradox.

We do not know exactly what variables are responsible for the health benefit that alcohol seems to offer. Moderate drinkers may have more relaxed lifestyles, or certain compounds in wine or whisky may contribute. But for men who go beyond two drinks a day, the risks of cancer, stroke and alcoholism all begin to rise. And while moderate drinking may be beneficial for some of us, it is most likely helpful only if we can afford the calories; and it is not advisable for those who have a problem controlling consumption. A drink a day also should not be used as an excuse to avoid other efforts to lower your risk of heart disease. And finally, women concerned about breast cancer should be aware that more than one drink per day may contribute to a greater risk of breast cancer.

Chapter 8

WHAT KIND OF WATER DO YOU DRINK? TAP WATER VERSUS BOTTLED OR FILTERED WATER

A REPORT FROM THE CITY OF NEW ORLEANS, IN THE MISSISSIPPI DELTA, rocked North America in 1974. The city's drinking water was found to have levels of carcinogenic chemicals sufficient to raise the incidence of kidney, bladder and urinary tract cancers significantly above such occurrences in other North American cities. Most cities do not have the extreme water problems of New Orleans, but many may come close. Tap water won't kill you instantly, but most municipally treated tap water is a cause for concern. Even the chlorine that is added to kill bacteria may be hazardous, and besides, it smells and tastes pretty terrible.

Municipal water is the cheapest source of drinking water, and most of it is bacteria free. However, depending on where you live, it can contain metals and all sorts of harmful chemicals, some of which are proven carcinogens. Chemical contaminants range from aluminum, to pesticides, to industrial toxins such as cleaning fluid.

Some of these contaminants appear to be associated with greater health consequences than has previously been thought. However, of the up to 60 substances commonly found in the drinking water that supplies large Canadian cities, guidelines for acceptable maximum levels have been assigned only to 17.

A City of Toronto report on its drinking water (Department of Public Health Technical Report, December 1990) concluded, "The state of our knowledge regarding a wide range of health hazards resulting from exposure to chemical contaminants, even at very low levels, is limited. Potential immunological and reproductive effects are not adequately considered ... Chemicals also may interact in the body in ways that we do not fully understand." In other words, acceptable levels of contaminants have been arbitrarily determined, and such standards may not be safe. Pollutants in tap water may combine with other environmental contaminants in

65

our bodies, making potential health hazards even more serious. Fifteen years after we first suspected such problems, we've done very little about them. In fact, some Great Lakes water quality improvement programs, which affect millions of North Americans, are up to nine years behind schedule!

There is not a great deal we can do to instantly limit our exposure to most sources of environmental pollution. However, for those of us who live in large metropolitan areas, avoiding tap water is fairly easy. Furthermore, I believe it is *essential* that our children do not drink it regularly, until it is further treated. But don't become paranoid. Dehydration is more harmful than the longer-term health effects of drinking an occasional glass of tap water. If you're thirsty and don't have an immediate alternative, by all means have some tap water.

Drinking water never used to be a chemical soup, but industry grew without strict laws governing waste disposal. Obviously pollution is worse in large cities and wherever water supplies are surrounded by concentrations of industry; water supplying cities and towns downstream will also be higher in pollutants.

We are now faced with a fairly universal problem, but without a universal solution. North American governments want their water supplies to be clean and healthy, but a major improvement is a far too expensive proposition, and implementation of broad legislative changes will take years. We, the end users, would pay dearly for significant improvements in drinking water because only 5% of the water that is municipally treated ends up being used for drinking or cooking. The rest is used for washing, watering the lawn and industrial purposes.

Two problems can be rectified easily, especially if you live in a house. The first is lead. Lead leaches into the water from the lead solder used in older plumbing joints. A 1992 study, published in the *New England Journal of Medicine*, recommends running the cold water tap in the morning for two minutes before drawing drinking water. This action drains the water that has been sitting in the pipes overnight accumulating lead.

A convenient alternative is to take a shower, flush the toilet, and run the water for about 30 seconds or till it is cold. Draining your pipes is especially important if you have young children or infants, who seem much more susceptible to lead poisoning than adults. Lead has been recently banned from plumbing solder.

The shower and flush method is not effective in apartment or office buildings, as early in the morning it would take a long time to flush pipes on higher floors. The water is probably okay by mid-morning. If you drink tap water, draw it late in the day. And keep a jug in the fridge; this also minimizes chlorine.

Chlorine is used to kill bacteria. Often so much chlorine is dumped into the water at the treatment plant that you can smell it when water is running. Chlorinated water has not yet been directly implicated in any health hazards, but chlorine can combine with other chemicals in the water to produce harmful compounds. Boiling water for one minute or leaving an opened container in the refrigerator will evaporate chlorine. Don't leave unchlorinated water in a warm place, as bacteria can breed.

Organic chemicals (PCBs, benzene and other industrially used compounds) and metals such as aluminum are more complicated problems. Until a Safe Drinking Water Act is implemented, the alternative to plain tap water (from high-risk sources) is filtering your tap water or using bottled water. Bottled water is expensive. Tests by the Toronto water study researchers showed some brands are not healthier than tap water, as they, too, may contain pollutants, and some of the chemicals in the plastic containers can also leach into the water. But major brands are generally healthier than tap water.

BOTTLED WATER

Here are some recommendations for bottled water:

- The best bottled water is spring water from a non-industrial area. The label should clearly state "Natural Spring Water Bottled from the Source," or some equivalent of this. "Spring Fresh," "Spring Type" and "Spring Pure" are all labelling ploys. Such descriptions can apply to tap or well water that has been minimally treated. Check the source of your water.
- To obtain independent information on water bottlers, write or call your provincial water bottlers association or the Canadian Water Quality Association.

- Obtain (preferably independent) current test data from your favourite bottler to ensure bacteria and harmful chemicals have been adequately treated, and make sure the water is not too high in minerals. All reputable bottlers test their water regularly and can provide this information.
- If the water tastes like plastic, request that the bottler rectify the situation by changing the containers used, or switch brands.
- Don't drink only mineral water. It can be dangerous to consume excessive quantities of trace minerals.
- Keep your water cooler disinfected and clean the neck of the bottle before submerging it in the reservoir of the cooler.
- Don't leave opened bottles of water in direct sunlight, as this encourages bacterial and algae growth.
- Bottled water in Ontario and many other parts of Canada is not fluoridated, but most bottled water in the United States is. Fluoride is absorbed only into young, growing teeth. Therefore there is no benefit to adults who drink fluoridated water. If you have kids who drink bottled water, dissolve a fluoride pill in the bottle before using it, or give your children fluoride supplements. Ask your pharmacist for details.

TREATED TAP WATER

Home water treatment devices are the other solution to tap water and are known as *point-of-use systems*. They are usually small appliances that fit onto a kitchen faucet or are attached to the cold water line under the sink. Another common point-of-use device is a pour-through system, in which water is manually poured through a filter into a storage container.

Point-of-use devices differ widely in their effectiveness in removing specific contaminants from the water. And the actual removal efficiency of a device will depend on its proper installation, operation and servicing. The two most common types of home treatment units are *activated carbon* and *reverse osmosis*.

Activated carbon filters are not efficient at removing most metals, but they do remove organic contaminants, such as industrial chemicals, and portions of some metals. In Toronto, for example, lead and aluminum are the most problematic metals. Some carbon filters will remove up to half of the aluminum, and a few brands also have a separate lead filter attached. Remember, the treated water that sits in the filter no longer contains chlorine and bacteria can therefore breed in it. To make sure that bacteria cannot grow in this water, check that the unit is labelled "bacteriostatic" and service it according to manufacturer's guidelines. Before drawing fresh water, run the water through the filter to flush that which has been standing in it.

Reverse osmosis units are more expensive than carbon filters. They are efficient at removing inorganic contaminants, including metals, but they do not remove many organic pollutants. When two or more treatment technologies, like reverse osmosis and carbon, are combined in the same system, the range of contaminants that can be removed becomes much broader.

HOW TO CHECK YOUR WATER

- Knowledgeable salespeople familiar with the contaminants in local water supplies can help you choose the most effective unit for your needs. Misrepresentation by salespeople and manufacturers is common in the water treatment business. Consult salespeople who represent various manufacturers. (See the Yellow Pages under Water Purification and Filtration.)
- In Canada, distribution of information on the quality of local drinking water is the responsibility of each treatment facility. Contact your local treatment facility for a list of the type and level of contaminants in the water. They also should be able to provide you with information about the favoured method for point-of-use treatment in your area. If they can't help you, Health and Welfare Canada will. Write to Health and Welfare Canada, Health Protection Branch, Environmental Health Directorate, Microbiology Advisor, Ottawa, Ontario K1A 0L2, (613)957-1505, for literature on the filtration abilities of water filters and answers to specific questions.
- A report by the United States General Accounting Office found that many states do not monitor local water quality closely enough, and not all contaminants present are tested for. So, to find out what kind of filter you need in the United States, call the Water Quality Association, at (312)369-1600, or the National Sanitation Foundation, at (313)769-8010.

Chapter 9
VITAMINS

VITAMINS ARE ORGANIC — THAT IS, CARBON-BASED — SUBSTANCES or nutrients needed for proper metabolic functioning. Vitamins prevent diseases of malnutrition and even help our hair, nails and skin to look better. We require very small amounts, but our bodies cannot manufacture most of them. They must come from the food we eat. Processed and prepared foods are not nearly as good sources of vitamins as fresh, raw or simply cooked foods, and supplements are not a substitute for a good diet.

To date, 13 vitamins are considered essential to our health: A, C, D, E, K and a group of eight vitamins called the B-complex — thiamine, riboflavin, niacin, B_6, pantothenic acid, biotin, folacin and B_{12}. Research involving vitamins and minerals has come a long way in the past 20 years. Studies that have examined the variety of ways vitamins contribute to our health have confirmed the benefits of vitamins in food; our food also provides other yet unspecified micro-nutrients, which we do not have the technology to put into pill form.

Unfortunately, when it comes to quick fixes that make us feel better, vitamin and mineral pills, together with a host of food supplements, take centre stage. Many of us would rather pop a pill than consider our level of stress, how often we sleep well (also a good indicator of other problems in our lives) and what we eat. We do this despite decades of pronouncements by our national health organizations emphasizing that a balanced diet provides us with all the nutrients we require. Warnings that vitamin supplements are not nearly as effective as vitamins that naturally occur in food, and that megadosing is unequivocally dangerous, do not seem to deter us. But instant solutions have long-term costs.

At a recent New York Academy of Science conference, financed in part by Hoffman-LaRoche, a pharmaceutical giant that makes highly profitable vitamin supplements, most researchers stated that their work did not advocate the use of vitamin tablets except in limited circumstances. The conclusion was that situations in which supplementing is effective are still a minor part of the picture, in that supplementing is not a substitution for a healthy diet. Most of the researchers were far more eager to emphasize the need to eat green, leafy vegetables, fruits and grains.

Testimonials of vitamin B restoring stamina are only true if someone had a vitamin B deficiency to begin with. Likewise, consulting a pseudo-medical practitioner who determines, for example, that your fatigue is due to a low level of pituitary hormone, and who prescribes a commercially available supplement of sheep brain tissue high in pituitary hormone, is the quickest route to an early grave. If you develop symptoms or suspect that you have a vitamin or mineral deficiency, consult a doctor. Noticing potential problems as early as possible and assessing them through traditional medical channels is the surest route to health and longevity. Alternative medicine can prove useful in treatment protocol, but accurate diagnosis is an essential first step.

THE DANGERS OF MEGADOSING

In all fairness to anyone who has attempted to understand the role of vitamins and minerals, some mainstream scientists have greatly complicated the issue by touting the miracles that supposedly occur when we raise Recommended Daily Allowances, or RDAs, several fold. For example, in 1970, despite ridicule by health authorities, the highly respected chemist Linus Pauling preached the virtues of vitamin C megadoses. Vitamin C has had so many claims made in its favour, how can we know what is true?

Let's dispel one myth immediately: megadosing can be dangerous. Most vitamins assist enzyme function in your body. To do so they must link up with certain proteins. By megadosing, you provide your body with more of a given vitamin than its available protein. Some excess vitamins are simply excreted, producing expensive urine with no added benefit. Excessive doses of other vitamins can be toxic. For example:

- Taking five times the RDA of vitamin A, more than 25,000 IU (International Units), can lead to liver damage, hair loss, blurred vision and headaches. One multi-vitamin often contains 10,000 IU, so overdosing is easy.
- High doses of vitamin C can produce stomach aches and diarrhea,

and may stress the kidneys, which flush the excess of this vitamin out of the body.

- Daily doses of more than 50,000 IU of vitamin D can lead to a build-up of calcium in the muscles, including the heart tissue. This can impede normal muscle function.
- More than 100 mg of iron taken daily can cause liver damage and excessive intake may also contribute to heart disease.

GUIDELINES FOR VITAMIN CONSUMPTION

Given the role that vitamins seem to play, what quantities should we consume? For the past 50 years, Recommended Daily Allowances, have guided our vitamin intake. These guidelines were introduced during World War II to ensure that soldiers didn't suffer from malnutrition. After the war the standards were applied to the general population. Further standards were later set for different sexes, age groups and special-needs groups such as pregnant women. In 1968, to simplify matters, the United States Food and Drug Administration (FDA) endorsed the highest standard, that for teenage boys, as the national standard. These are now the numbers you see on food labels.

Every five years the more detailed list of standards is updated and most nutritionists draw on the updated list when working with people. Both sets of standards allow a comfortable margin of nutritional safety when considering common diseases of vitamin deficiency. Most North Americans do not consume enough vitamins to meet the guidelines, but still do not develop vitamin-deficiency diseases like scurvy, beriberi and night blindness.

In 1993 the FDA intends to average the RDAs for the various groups to make a new standard. The new figures (Reference Daily Intakes or RDIs) will be considerably lower than current recommendations. For example, vitamins A, B, C and E and the mineral iron will be reduced anywhere from 10 to 80%, in the belief that current numbers are too high for the average person.

The new standard is based solely upon the amount of vitamins required to prevent vitamin deficiencies. However, research suggests one person's need for a vitamin is not the same as the next person's. Adults older than 60 may need 30% more vitamin B_6 than young adults, as they may no longer process this vitamin as efficiently. Also, anti-inflammatories and diuretics, commonly prescribed to older people, can hinder vitamin absorption, requiring higher RDAs.

Vitamins do much more than prevent malnutrition, as dozens of recent findings indicate. For example, we have long known that vitamin C prevents scurvy when 60 mg is consumed daily. But vitamin C has been shown to protect against cataracts and cancer when the RDA is raised to at least 100 mg. And vitamin E appears to have disease-preventing properties when the RDA is raised from 10 or 15 IU to 400 IU.

Nutritionists and doctors agree that almost everyone's basic vitamin needs can be met by eating a diet rich in fruit, vegetables and grains. But we don't need to eat buckets of vegetables to meet our daily requirements. The new Canada Food Guide will be similar to the U.S. government's 1992 dietary guidelines. The latter urges a varied daily meal plan, which is not as ambitious as it might first appear. For one thing, a serving size is a fairly small portion. Here are the guidelines — and an example of one serving:

- 2 to 3 dairy servings — 1 serving = 1 cup milk
- 3 to 5 servings of vegetables — 1 serving = ½ cup
- 2 to 4 servings of fruit — 1 serving = ½ cup or 1 small piece
- 6 to 11 servings of breads, rice, pasta and grains — 1 serving = 1 slice of bread, 1 small potato or ½ cup rice or pasta
- 2 to 3 servings of meat, eggs, poultry, fish and dried beans — 1 meat serving = 2 to 3 oz

Although 6 to 11 servings of bread, rice, pasta or grain may be more than some people can comfortably consume, the recommendations together make three square meals a day. Surprisingly, most people don't even come close to this consumption. According to the National Centre for Health Statistics in the United States, only 9% of North Americans have five servings of fruit and vegetables each day. Many of us need to improve our general eating patterns.

GETTING THE MOST NUTRIENTS OUT OF YOUR FOOD
- Cooked food does not have the same amount of water-soluble vitamins as fresh, uncooked, unprocessed food. Buy fresh or frozen fruits and vegetables rather than canned. And try to buy

vine-ripened fruits and vegetables, as these have the most vitamins in them.

- To prevent withering, refrigerate vegetables in your crisper in
  air-tight bags.
- If you must use food from cans, rinse the contents quickly with
  water to remove the salty brine. If possible, store cans below
  18°C (65°F) to minimize vitamin loss.
- Store all foods, including those you ripen yourself, away from
  strong sunlight.
- Wrap all leftovers in air-tight wrapping.
- Don't soak fresh vegetables when cleaning them, and don't store
  cut-up vegetables in water, as vitamins leach out. Do not cut
  vegetables into small pieces ahead of time, as they lose vitamin
  C. If you find that you prepare vegetables ahead of time and
  store them as your snack food, store them in water, then save
  the water for soup recipes and sauces.
- Steam or bake vegetables, instead of boiling them. (Boiling causes vitamins to escape.) Steaming in the microwave requires
  almost no water and is the best way to retain vitamins.
- Keep cooking times as short as possible. Eat raw fruits and vegetables when possible.
- The skins of fruits and vegetables contain lots of vitamins and
  fibre. Cook vegetables with the skins on, and eat the skins of
  fruits. To remove herbicides, fungicides and pesticides from the
  surface, use a fruit and vegetable safety rinse like Dr. Browner's,
  which can be found in health food stores.

WHEN IS IT APPROPRIATE TO SUPPLEMENT WITH VITAMINS?

Try to get all of the RDA for each nutrient daily, but don't worry
if on a particular day you fall above or below the requirement, or
if you eat the odd junk-food meal. If you eat a healthy diet, unless
you fall into any of the groups listed below, your intake will average out properly.

- *Junk eaters, those who eat mainly packaged, processed foods and those
  not eating a varied, well-balanced diet.* Vitamins work with other
  nutrients in food. They cannot replace food or turn a junk-food

diet into a healthy one. Junk eaters will benefit from a daily multi-vitamin — but don't fool yourself. If you fall into this group, you are susceptible to so many other health risks that supplementing alone is not sufficient.

- *Pregnant women.* If you are not eating a healthy diet, or if morning sickness reduces your consumption of food, take a daily supplement formulated for pregnant women. It is essential not to megadose, as this can lead to birth defects.
- *Those suffering from premenstrual syndrome* seem to feel better when taking up to 50 mg of B_6 and a multi-B complex daily. Be sure that total B_6 intake does not exceed 50 mg.
- *Those consuming less than 1,200 calories per day.* If you are physically active, you should take a multi-vitamin.
- *Strict vegans.* A vegan is a vegetarian who does not ingest any type of animal protein. You probably should take a daily B_{12} supplement, unless you are sure that your B_{12} intake is sufficient.
- *The elderly.* Many elderly people reduce their consumption of healthy food or the variety of food they consume. These people should supplement with a multi-vitamin and consult a qualified nutritionist for more specific guidance.
- *Frequent aspirin takers.* Aspirin interferes with the metabolism of vitamin C and folacin (a member of the vitamin B family). Consult with your doctor about use of supplements.
- *Heavy drinkers, smokers and those under prolonged stress.* All these people may be deficient in vitamins B and C. They are also significantly more susceptible to developing several diseases and disorders. Vitamin supplementation on its own isn't a solution. Nevertheless, I recommend a daily vitamin B complex and a 500 mg vitamin C supplement. Vitamin C should contain bioflavinoids, which help its absorption. To ensure small amounts are made available through the day, buy time-released brands of both C and B vitamins.
- *Endurance athletes* often require additional sodium, potassium, calcium and most vitamins. Such people should eat to win and consult a nutritionist about moderate supplementing.
- *Those frequently tired during the day.* If you get adequate sleep and your medical exam is okay but you are still tired, you could be slightly vitamin deficient and may benefit from a multi-vitamin.

- *Surgery patients* may have increased needs for vitamin C, E and the B complex. If your doctor does not consider it a conflict, supplement with a time-released B complex and C, E and beta carotene for one week before and at least six weeks after major surgery. Ask your doctor for recommended dosages.
- *Prolonged users of antibiotics.* Antibiotics destroy the good bacteria that live in your intestinal tract. I recommend *Lactobacillus Acidophilus* — the live kind found in tablets in the refrigerator at health food stores — to replace this bacteria. Don't worry that you are eating bacteria; it's good bacteria, similar to that in yogurt.

THE NEW VITAMIN RESEARCH

Today's scientists suspect that traditional medical views of vitamins and minerals are too limited. Vitamins were once thought necessary to combat nutritional deficiencies, such as scurvy and rickets. It wasn't until the 1970s that we discovered a broader link between diet and health. This knowledge led to a renewed effort to analyze each nutrient that we eat to learn its specific benefits.

It was through this effort that we discovered, in the late 1980s, the role of vitamins in protecting against many diseases. Many ills — from birth defects and cataracts to heart disease and cancer — now appear to be at least partly vitamin related. And an increasingly strong case is being developed for the role of vitamins in assuring optimal health and vitality.

The new era of vitamin studies began when scientists realized that people in Japan and other countries who generally eat low-fat foods rich in vitamins often live longer and experience fewer chronic diseases than those who limit their intake of vitamin-rich vegetables. For example, an analysis of 15 studies involving vitamin C found a significant benefit from eating foods rich in vitamin C, among them citrus fruits, melons, tomatoes and green vegetables. The people who ate a diet rich in these foods experienced only half to a third of the esophagus and stomach cancer rates found in those who ate very little of these foods.

Are these benefits attributable to the vitamins themselves? Or are there other substances present in the foods? We don't know yet. Remember, though, such low-fat foods are also high in fibre, carbohydrates and proteins. When put into powders and pills, nutrients become a very costly, tasteless substitute for food and may lack important substances that we cannot yet synthesize.

Although evidence is still preliminary, most of the vitamin excitement revolves around a group of vitamins — C, E and beta carotene — and a mineral called selenium. These are known as antioxidants and are abundant in fruits, vegetables and grains. They seem to neutralize and remove certain molecules called free radicals. Free radicals are a byproduct of normal metabolism, and excessively high levels are related to a high consumption of fat. They are also created by exposure to X-rays, surgery and injury, sunlight, ozone, tobacco smoke, car exhaust and other pollutants. These unstable molecules damage DNA, alter biochemical compounds and kill cells outright. They have been implicated in the development of cancer, cataracts (a clouding of the eye), and heart and lung disease. Free radicals may also contribute to the gradual deterioration that is part of ageing.

Studies show that vitamins C and E reduce the risks of cataracts by one half. Vitamin E may help prevent free radicals from injuring the heart and help boost immune functioning in healthy older people. The effects of air pollution are chronic, and E also may turn out to be a potent lung saver.

In a large-population 10-year study, doctors at Harvard Medical School found that men with a history of cardiac disease suffered half the number of heart attacks, strokes and deaths when given 50 mg daily supplements of beta carotene. Beta carotene may prove to be effective in combating cancer as well.

In women, folic acid, a B vitamin, seems to guard against the two most common neurological birth defects (spina bifida and anencephaly), as well as cervical cancer. A small study at the University of California at Berkeley indicated that low vitamin C levels in men may damage their sperm and thereby lead to birth defects. Until recently, men's diet and smoking habits were not believed to affect their offspring. Smokers in the study were at particular risk, as cigarette smoking lowers vitamin C. Researchers found a higher incidence of leukemia and lymphoma in the children of these men.

ANTIOXIDANT FOODS

The Brassica family of vegetables contains a substance called an indole, which has antioxidant properties. These vegetables include broccoli, Brussels sprouts, cabbage and cauliflower. Fruits and vegetables high in vitamin C also display anti-carcinogenic properties. And whole grains and vegetable oils contain vitamin E, which is an antioxidant.

Those who eat a healthy, balanced diet get considerably more than the recommended daily intake of beta carotene and vitamin C. However, vitamin E consumption, especially for those who watch their fat intake, is often below that required to have an antioxidant effect. As it appears that vitamin E enhances immune functioning, current research suggests that supplementing with up to 400 IU per day is safe and effective. We do not yet have enough information to go beyond these general recommendations.

WHAT BRAND OF VITAMIN PILLS SHOULD I BUY?

To be effective, vitamin pills must be properly manufactured. But even if we can figure out the best dose, we don't always know what to make of manufacturers' claims about things such as "proven release" or "high absorbency." Pricing also can be arbitrary; the most expensive may not be the best. They may simply have the largest advertising budget, and most advertising messages are groundless.

Although there are differences in how well various brands of vitamins assimilate into your body, surveys that provide such information are out of date. For now we have to buy on faith. Stick with reputable stores and the more natural brands (without fillers and binders) that have the best reputations.

Certain harmful effects can occur even with short-term over-supplementing. So until all the data are in, the wisest choice is to double your efforts to eat a healthy diet. Above all, remember that happiness is enjoying your vices in moderation. No matter how powerful antioxidants and other nutrients turn out to be, they will never be a substitute for eating well.

Chapter 10
MINERALS

THERE ARE MORE THAN 60 MINERALS IN THE BODY, 22 OF THEM ESSEN-
tial. However, it would not be surprising if the list was to grow as
we learn more about minerals. The optimal daily consumption
for some minerals is still a matter of debate, and RDAs exist for
only seven minerals. Five others have what we call "estimated safe
and adequate daily intakes." Note that women require higher daily
amounts of some minerals than do men.

Although research continues, it is now clear that minerals, like
vitamins, are essential to a host of vital body processes. Deficiencies
of various minerals appear to play a role in the development of
cardiovascular disease, mature-onset diabetes, high blood pressure and cancer. Whereas a healthy diet provides most of us with
all the minerals we need, it is more difficult to consume and absorb
adequate quantities of zinc, calcium, and iron than other essential
nutrients.

ZINC
A zinc deficiency can delay puberty, impair wound healing and
lead to fetal abnormalities. Food loses considerable amounts of
zinc during processing. Oysters, crab meat, beef, eggs, poultry,
brewers yeast and whole wheat bread are good sources of zinc.

CALCIUM
Calcium is required for bone development, blood clotting, muscle contraction and nerve transmission. Calcium deficiencies are
much more common in women than in men. The typical North
American woman consumes less than half the calcium she requires
each day! There are no obvious symptoms of calcium deficiency,
besides possibly having white spots on your fingernails and toe-
nails, or muscle cramps in your legs.

During the first 20 to 30 years of life, our bones develop with
the aid of the calcium we consume. And we store about 90% of
our body's calcium in our bones. Beginning in adolescence, many
people reduce their intake of calcium-rich dairy products and, to

make matters worse, often consume soft drinks in place of milk. The phosphates in the soft drinks leach calcium out of the system. We should either stop drinking soft drinks or consume no more than two cans a day.

After the age of about 50, to meet some of its needs, the body absorbs part of its bone mass, and the bone mass begins to decline. The reabsorption of calcium from our bones is not a problem for those who had adequate calcium intake during the first 30 years of their lives. Others, however, are at a risk of developing osteoporosis. This condition of weak and brittle bones and shrinkage in stature is irreversible.

As we age, our ability to absorb calcium diminishes from 75% to only 15%, so we cannot build our bones back up. There is no evidence that calcium supplements taken at this stage of life can compensate for a lifetime of deficiency. They can help only to prevent further damage.

To build and maintain bone density, consume adequate amounts of both vitamin D and calcium. Low-fat milk, yogurt and cheese (except cottage cheese, which is a comparatively inferior source of calcium) are excellent sources of both minerals. These dairy sources also contain nutrients that aid calcium absorption. Leafy green vegetables, tofu and canned salmon or sardines with the bones left in are other good sources of calcium.

Some foods are fortified with calcium. However, the amount of calcium absorbed from these fortified foods is yet to be determined. While some of them may be healthy, I wouldn't spend extra money for them because of their calcium content. On the other hand, if you take calcium supplements, note that more expensive supplements do not seem to be absorbed more readily than a simple dose of calcium carbonate. (To enhance absorption, take the supplement with meals.) But don't overdo it — follow recommended doses. Overdosing on calcium can cause calcium kidney stones. Finally, to help increase the strength of your bones, engage in regular weight-bearing exercise, such as walking.

The following people should take calcium carbonate as a daily supplement:
• *Pregnant women*. It is essential that they get enough calcium. If they are lactose intolerant or dislike milk, a supplement should

be taken to ensure an intake of 1,200 mg of calcium daily. This is the equivalent of 4 cups of milk. Yogurt and cheese are calcium-rich alternatives.

• *Women who are no longer menstruating, not taking estrogen replacements and not consuming dairy products.* Post-menopausal women should consume a total of 1,200 to 1,500 mg of calcium per day. This amount is rarely consumed by such women.

• *Anyone who consumes a lot of caffeine, alcohol or protein* should supplement with 650 mg of calcium per day to replace the calcium that is leached out of the system.

• *Those who are lactose intolerant and who are not eating alternative calcium-rich foods* should supplement with 650 mg per day.

IRON

If you eat a healthy diet and do not fall into any of the special-needs groups listed below, you probably don't need an iron supplement. Iron and calcium are the two minerals in which women are most often deficient. Up to 15% of North American women of child-bearing age have some form of iron deficiency. Often the first stage of iron deficiency has no symptoms.

If you suspect that you are anemic because you frequently feel tired or eat an unhealthy diet, consult a doctor. The RDAs for iron, as of mid-1992, are:

Age	Iron (mg)
less than 6 months	10
6 months to 3 years	15
4 to 10 years	10
11 to 18 years	15
19 to 50 years (men)	10
(women)	15
over 51 years	10

If you supplement with iron and calcium, to maximize iron absorption do not take your iron supplement with your calcium supplement or with food such as a dairy product. The following groups may not consume enough iron despite eating a balanced diet:

• *Menstruating women.* If such women eat 1,500 calories per day of a typical unhealthy North American diet, they consume only half of their iron requirement. Women who bleed heavily should pay extra attention to their iron intake.

• *Dieters, especially women.* Those consuming a diet of less than 1,200 calories may have trouble getting enough iron.

• *Pregnant women* must supplement with iron and continue the supplements for two to three months after childbirth, as they would typically have to eat more than 4,000 calories a day to meet the requirement for this mineral. Consult with a physician for details.

• *Endurance athletes* have a higher incidence of iron depletion than the general population. Regular monitoring is prudent.

• *Those who don't eat red meat* would be wise to monitor iron levels periodically. Beef, pork and lamb are among the richest sources of easily absorbable iron. The iron in vegetables, grains and beans is not absorbed nearly as well, although if you typically eat a diet rich in these food sources you should not have an iron deficiency.

• *Infants, children and teenagers.* Rapid growth considerably increases iron demands. The person most at risk is a menstruating adolescent who is still growing but who is not eating properly.

• *Those who consume a lot of soft drinks.* These drinks contribute excess phosphorus to the diet. This interferes with iron absorption and is a major concern for heavy pop drinkers under 30 years of age. Limit consumption of pop to two cans a day and don't use it as a substitute for dairy products.

Consuming foods that are high in vitamin C along with those high in iron can double or triple iron absorption. Tomatoes, sweet peppers, broccoli, cauliflower, leafy greens and potatoes with the skins on are good sources of vitamin C. A variety of processed foods, such as bread, cereal and pasta, are iron enriched. Peas, beans and corn, while not nearly as good as lean red meat, are comparatively good plant sources of iron. These are the same foods that are high in vitamins, fibre and complex carbohydrates. Finally, note that the oxalic acid in spinach inhibits iron absorption, and so does drinking coffee or tea during or immediately after a meal.

VITAMIN AND MINERAL SUPPLEMENTS

It is not my intention in this book to demean age-old non-Western herbal remedies. I do not profess to be an expert in such alternative medicines. But herbal wisdom aside, vitamins and minerals are the nutrients most commonly found in "miracle cures" and "wonder supplements."

There are no legally enforceable regulations controlling recommended doses or the manufacturing of food supplements. This means that although "alternative" remedies can be quite useful, in certain situations some supplements can be harmful to your health. They may contain impurities, or the recommended dose may be too high. Con artists will try to pass off variations of ancient remedies as wonder cures. For example, young ginseng is not nearly as potent as older roots, although it is often marketed as being very potent.

If such supplements seem to help you, it may be that you are lacking in an essential vitamin or mineral contained in the supplement. You may not need all the ingredients the supplement's label claims is in it. And the essential vitamin or mineral can usually be provided more safely, effectively and economically by dietary change, a multi-vitamin or a specific mineral supplement. Furthermore, excess consumption of some minerals can be just as dangerous as vitamin megadoses. If you want to increase your daily consumption of minerals, don't waste your money on miracle cures — improve your diet.

If you suspect that you may have special needs, a doctor can authorize a simple blood test to determine your specific requirements and then show you how to supplement wisely. For example, pregnant women who suffer from nausea benefit from one gram of powdered gingerroot (in capsules) each day. This well-researched supplementing approach can be recommended by a doctor.

Part II
MAKING SMART CHOICES

The first part of this book armed you with information about the food you eat. You now know enough to be flexible about your diet. And personal choice is essential if your diet is to be healthy and balanced. With a little practice of the basics, you'll find that sensible decisions become second nature, no matter where you are — or so it would seem.

But sometimes we do not have control over what food we choose. Advertisers have tremendous latitude in what they say, and often essential nutritional information is hidden from us. The process of reading food product labels is like learning to crack a secret code. Once we understand the code, we have all the information we need to make healthy choices. In Chapter 11, I teach you how to read the product labels.

What should we do when someone else prepares our meals for us? In today's fast-paced world, many of us often eat away from home. At restaurants the food depends on the chef, and at parties or on airplanes we are at the mercy of a set menu. But selections are not as limited as they may appear. In Chapter 12 are guidelines that will enable you to make smart choices no matter where you are.

Common wisdom tells us to exercise, because exercise provides several health-related benefits, such as a stronger heart and lower cholesterol. The vast majority of people who achieve and maintain a healthy body weight do so through a combination of healthy eating and regular exercise. And most of those who lose weight but who do not exercise do not maintain their weight loss. Exercise makes us feel great because it stimulates the secretion of hormones that elevate our mood. This uplifting energy gives us the motivation to take care of our nutritional needs and provides the will-power to see us through temptation. In Chapter 13, I offer an intelligent approach to exercise. Exercise is easy, and when done properly, it's not painful.

Chapter 11

UNDERSTANDING LABELS

READING FOOD LABELS IS LIKE BREAKING A SECRET CODE. ONCE YOU understand the code, you can breeze through your shopping. You will remember superior brands and be able to skim new labels quickly. Advertisers are playing with your health when they design labels. The first thing to appreciate is that government standards for food labelling are inadequate and incomplete. (In the United States, several changes that would provide more detail on labels are under discussion.)

Don't assume that someone is looking out for your health. Toxic metals are no longer present in food, but with the rapid growth of processed foods since 1960, foods contain a wide range of new chemical additives. Current testing procedures are limited, so it is impossible to guarantee the effects of these chemicals. Many substances once thought to be safe are now under evaluation.

Some manufacturers provide more information on their labels than the law requires, and they use superior-quality ingredients with a minimum of additives. But legislation allows unscrupulous manufacturers to get away with murder — pun intended! To get a better understanding of the current situation, let's break the label code one item at a time. First comes the number of grams of protein, carbohydrate and fat and the percentage of calories contained in these three sources. Second is the list of ingredients. And last is the meaning of descriptive words such as "lite" and "natural."

WHERE THE CALORIES COME FROM

Food labels provide nutrients in grams, but they rarely tell us the percentage of calories that come from fat. However, the number of grams of protein, carbohydrate and fat can be used to find the percentage of calories from each source. Remember, proteins and carbohydrates both have four calories per gram, and fats have nine. So the number of grams of each nutrient in a given food and the percentage of calories from each source will not be the same.

As an example, consider All-Natural, No-Cholesterol Oat Puffs. The manufacturer states on the label that one serving has

Energy	80 calories
Protein	1 gram
Carbohydrate	8 grams
Fat	5 grams

It seems that there are more grams of carbohydrate than anything else in this snack food, and that it would be a healthy choice. But let's look more closely and calculate how many calories each source provides.

Protein: 1 gram x 4 cal/gram = 4 calories from protein
Carbohydrate: 8 grams x 4 cal/gram = 32 calories from carbohydrate
Fat: 5 grams x 9 cal/gram = 45 calories from fat

Out of 80 total calories, 45, or 55%, come from fat ($45 \div 80$ x 100 = 55%). As is so common with snack foods, this snack is more than one-half fat!

What about carbohydrates and protein? The snack is 40% carbohydrate ($32 \div 80$ x 100 = 40%). The remaining portion, 5%, is protein. Snack foods are high in fat because they usually contain oil, which is a fat. And if the label says "may contain one or more of the following oils," rest assured that the more unhealthy type is used, as it is usually the cheapest.

There are two types of carbohydrates, simple (sugars) and complex (fruits, vegetables and whole grains that contain fibre). A label may have two carbohydrate categories, "Simple Sugars" and "Complex Carbohydrates." You should minimize your consumption of simple carbohydrates and eat more complex carbohydrates. To find how much of each carbohydrate source is in a product, multiply the grams of each carbohydrate by 4. If the label does not list the two types, look to see which ingredient comes first, sugar or a grain. Ingredients are listed in descending order by weight.

You can apply the formula to any food. Remember, your goal is to eat 30% or less of your daily calories from fat, 55% from mainly complex carbohydrates and 15% from protein.

Now consider the serving size of the All-Natural, No-Cholesterol Oat Puffs. The manufacturer stated on the label that one serving has 80 calories, but lists only nine puffs as a serving. Often manufacturers will list unrealistically small serving sizes to downplay the amount of calories, fat, sugar and salt in a product. So if you eat twice as much as the suggested serving size, multiply the number of calories from fat, carbohydrate and protein by 2 to see how many calories you are eating from each source.

The only exceptions to the formula are meat, milk and milk products such as yogurt and cheese. Labels on these products frequently don't list grams of protein, carbohydrate and fat. Therefore, we can't determine the percent of calories that come from fat. For example, 2% milk does not contain 2% of its calories as fat — 37% of its calories are from fat. The "2%" refers to the amount of fat by weight or volume. One percent milk gets 22% of its total calories from fat, and skim milk derives 5% of total calories from fat. Stay away from homogenized milk, as 45% of its calories are from fat. And cream is even worse.

Yogurt labels are the same as milk labels. But making substitutions is easy, as there are fat-free yogurts available. And they taste just as good as the higher-fat choices. In most situations I also find yogurt to be a great substitute for sour cream, which is high in fat. (Check the dip recipes on pages 148 to 151 for some ideas.)

The fat contained in cheese is indicated by a percentage followed by "MF," "MG" or "BF," depending on the country in which the cheese is manufactured. Cheese labelled 15% MF, MG or BF means that it, like milk, is 15% fat *by weight*. The label does not tell what percentage of the calories derive from fat. Here are some tips:

- Check the label for grams of fat per ounce. Fifteen percent MF or lower is a low-fat cheese, with 4 or 5 grams of fat per ounce. Regular cheeses, which average 35% MF, average 9 grams of fat per ounce.
- One ounce of regular cheese contains about 110 calories. It derives 81 of these calories from fat (9 grams of fat x 9 calories/gram = 81 calories, and 81÷110 x 100 = 73.6% fat). A

35% MF cheese, like Cheddar, is almost 74% fat. And that favourite Brie? It's more than 80% fat!

• Part-skim or "low-fat" cheese is a better choice, but it is not as low in fat as advertisers would like us to believe. It has about 75 calories and 4 to 5 grams of fat per ounce. So it is typically 48 to 60% fat. This percentage is in keeping with the protein-to-fat ratios that we find in lean animal meat, like the white meat of chicken. In an otherwise low-fat diet, low-fat cheese provides a good source of nutrients. There are now many varieties of low-fat cheeses on the market. Look for them or ask your grocer to carry a selection.

• Finally, I hate to break this to you, but cream cheese is not cheese, and it's 90% fat. Advertising that compares it to butter is misleading. The ads compare one teaspoon of cream cheese to one of butter. But who uses just one teaspoon of cream cheese? Well, you should. One *tablespoon* of cream cheese is 45 calories. Although the "light" versions are 30 calories, they are still quite high in fat.

The fat listed on meat labels also can be confusing. Ground meat labelled "75% lean" is not low in fat, although the label implies that the meat is only 25% fat. Again, the figure refers to the percentage of fat by weight, which is very different from the percentage of calories from fat. But here you cannot figure out what percent of calories come from fat unless the label provides total calories and grams of fat per ounce, or the percentage of calories provided by fat. The "75% lean" hamburger still derives about two-thirds of its calories from fat, and "extra-lean" hamburger is about half fat. This is one reason I recommend reducing red meat consumption.

THE LIST OF INGREDIENTS

The next part of the label is the list of ingredients. About 300 common products — for example ketchup, peanut butter and Cheddar cheese — legally do not have to have ingredients listed, although this situation probably will change. Most manufacturers do, however, list ingredients, and others will provide such information on request. Also note that the cholesterol content does not have to be provided unless a claim is made about it.

The name of a product does not necessarily have anything to do with the amount of that ingredient in the product. Ingredients are listed by weight, beginning with the one in the greatest quantity. If you check labels, you may be surprised to find out how many products are mainly oil, sugar or water. If oil appears at the beginning of the list, the product has more oil in it than any other ingredient. Oil is fat. To find how much fat the product contains, apply my formula. And remember that most processed products contain some oil, so look for the two healthy types —mono- and polyunsaturated oil.

The most common trick in ingredient lists is to hide the total amount of sugar in a food. Again, if calories from simple and complex carbohydrates appear on the label, by using my formula you can easily determine the percentage of calories from sugar versus those from complex carbohydrates. If the label does not list complex carbohydrates, sugar is usually the main source of carbohydrate. But to avoid listing sugar first, manufacturers list each type of sugar separately (such as liquid invert sugar, molasses, corn syrup solids, fructose, glucose and anything else ending in "-ose"). Separating the sugars into their generic names makes a food that is largely sugar appear to be otherwise.

Usually, chemicals like flavouring, spices and colouring, as well as preservatives and emulsifiers, appear last. Flavouring, colours and spices do not have to be listed by name. They can simply be called "natural flavouring" or "artificial colouring." Most preservatives, thickening agents and emulsifiers are considered safe, but some preservatives, such as BHA and BHT, are suspected carcinogens, and are under review.

However, the methods by which many chemicals have become regarded as safe cannot yet be proven to be scientifically sound. It's best to avoid or minimize consumption of food with a lot of chemicals in it. We subject ourselves to more than enough health hazards from situations that we cannot control. This one we can act on. Besides, foods containing several chemical flavourings and preservatives are usually highly processed, fattening and have little fibre in them.

THERE'S MORE TO A NAME THAN MEETS THE EYE

Because most people don't read the label, the third common ploy to keep us from realizing what we are eating is to give a product a healthy-sounding name. "Light" olive oil, "natural" potato chips and even "honey oat" cereal are typical examples. To break the final part of the code, we need to consider two things. The first part is terms like "light" and "natural" and the second is the name of the food.

Initially, the word "light" or "lite" meant calorie-reduced. But there is no legal definition of these words. "Light" can refer to light in colour or taste or to a light, fluffy texture. For example, "light" olive oil may not taste as strong as other olive oils, but it has the same number of calories and the same amount of fat. Only when meat and poultry are labelled "light" must they contain 25% less fat than the regular counterpart.

Several terms and descriptions are commonly used to describe products. "Low-calorie" means that the product contains no more than 40 calories per serving and less than 0.4 calories per gram. A maximum caloric count per gram prevents manufacturers from calling products with unrealistically small serving sizes "low-calorie." "Reduced-calorie" means that the item contains at least one-third less calories than an equivalent serving of the food that it imitates.

But "low-calorie" and "reduced-calorie" do not tell you how many calories come from fat, and many dietetic foods that are lower in calories are still high in fat. Fat often replaces sugar, so the product is less healthy than if the sugar was left in. Similarly, "dietetic" foods may be sugar-free or low in sodium, although this does not guarantee their health status, either. "Sugar-free" and "sugarless" mean no sucrose or table sugar has been added, but honey, glucose and fructose may still be added.

"Unsweetened" denotes that no sugar is added, and the better fruit juices are unsweetened. But fruit is high in natural sugar, and although it's a source of vitamins and minerals, when fruit is made into juice it does not have any fibre to help regulate the increase in our blood sugar. Fruit *drinks* contain only 10 to 34% fruit. The rest is water, sugar, colour, and flavouring. "Fruit-flavoured" means less than 10% real fruit — and usually none at all. If you drink juice, choose unsweetened fruit juice, frozen from concentrate, frozen reconstituted or fresh.

Products labelled "cholesterol-free" may have never contained cholesterol to begin with. But "cholesterol-free" salad dressings, crackers and cookies may be high in saturated fat.

Another common trick is to call a food "natural" or "organic." These foods are sometimes not processed, sometimes do not have any pesticides in them and may not contain additives. But there are no legal definitions of the terms, and producer-supported policing bodies do not immediately catch all infringements, so anything goes. Only meat or poultry labelled "natural" is minimally processed and free of artificial ingredients.

"Natural" potato chips are still potatoes and oil, and therefore are mostly fat. And the "organic" cookies and crackers sold in health food stores can be loaded with oil, salt and sugar. Granola, granola bars and trail mixes, even though they are often called "health" foods or "all natural," are also full of calories, fat and sugar (remember, it's not incorrect to call fat and sugar "natural"). New, healthier versions of these products are appearing on the shelves, and you can easily identify them by reading the labels.

"Healthy" is an undefined term that is overused on packages. Some consumer groups are lobbying the government to ban it from all packaged food. Advertisers also like to use minor ingredients in the names of products; they find that it makes their products more appealing. Imagine if car manufacturers could do this. "For sale: Volkswagen Beetle with mega horsepower." The VW Beetle had only about 50 horsepower. Such an ad would be equivalent to the description of a commercially prepared beef and bean burrito I recently came across — with only seven beans in it. Or "buttermilk" pancakes that I found, with less than one teaspoon of buttermilk in three pancakes. Then there's "whole wheat bread" with more white, refined flour than whole wheat flour. The list goes on and on.

"Enriched" flour may be vitamin B enriched, but the fibre lost during refining is not restored. "Fortified" foods may be selectively fortified with one vitamin — an expensive way to get a vitamin — but may be lacking in other vitamins and minerals that are lost during processing.

One kind of product that is rarely discussed is the medicinally oriented product, for example herbal tea. Herbs are frequently used as alternatives to prescription drugs, and most prescription drugs are made from herbs. But there is no authority that regulates the use of herbs in their natural forms. Labels on herbal products do not have to provide warnings of possible side effects. For example, laxative teas, diuretic teas and herbal supplements can be dangerous if consumed in large quantities, and some herbs can trigger allergic reactions. The packages of reputable companies will clearly state any side effects. If a label is uninformative, do not use the product. Write the manufacturer for more information, or consult a pharmacist, nutritionist or doctor.

Although healthy alternatives are coming to the market, I cannot emphasize strongly enough that the labels of most prepared and processed foods, from cereals to frozen dinners to spaghetti sauces to snack foods, use tricks to fool us. I can't provide you with a list of every item to avoid, but you now know why I say read the label. With very little practice you will be able to find the best brands. You also will come to know very quickly which manufacturers care about your health.

OTHER RECOMMENDATIONS

- Try to buy your fresh produce on the day it's delivered to the store. The store manager can give you a schedule.
- Ask whether the store buyer is personally familiar with manufacturers, or supports their reputation on hearsay alone.
- Do not eat an overly restricted diet. Variety will limit your exposure to particular additives and substandard products.
- Minimize your consumption of foods containing food colouring, and try not to eat too many cured meats, which contain nitrates and nitrites. These substances were carcinogenic when tested on animals.
- Be wary of product endorsements. They too are misleading. Snicker's chocolate bars and Wonder Bread may be the "official" chocolate bar and bread of the Olympics, but they are no healthier for it. The difficult part of this con game is convincing your kids that it's a ploy.

- Food additives have been implicated in hyperactivity and learning problems in children. Such difficulties may be more significantly related to the junk-food diet that results when labels and claims related to processed foods are taken at face value.
- As of mid-1992, irradiated food has not been proven safe, although some irradiated products may begin to show up on supermarket shelves. Such products must bear the "Radura" symbol. ☻ Until they are proved safe, I would suggest you avoid or minimize consumption of these products.

Chapter 12
EATING AWAY FROM HOME

Most of us eat out sometimes, in restaurants and fast-food joints, at parties and while travelling. It's difficult in these circumstances to control the menu and portion size. The tips and exercises in this chapter are for general application, things to do to avoid "eating with abandon."

RESTAURANTS

You find yourself at your favourite restaurant. You've been eating healthfully for a few months now and have not yet confronted a true pigging-out situation. Your companion goes for prime rib with all the trimmings, and another friend orders beef Wellington. You're salivating as the moment of decision arrives and the server asks to take your order.

Do you choose grilled fish, salad with dressing on the side and a baked potato with low-fat toppings, or go for broke? Surveys show that 70% of us go for it. Twelve ounces of prime beef, a baked potato with sour cream, buttered broccoli and a salad with Russian or blue cheese dressing comes in at about 1,800 calories, and is 73% fat.

When the menu comes up full of cream sauces and deep-fried delicacies, I solicit the help of my server. I ask for a poached or broiled entree without oil and for steamed vegetables. And I request sauces and salad dressing on the side.

Some servers are perfectly accustomed to healthy eating and accommodate a patron without a second thought. Others are more sympathetic if you tell them you're on a doctor's low-fat, low-cholesterol diet, rather than saying you simply want to lose some weight or just eat more healthfully.

If being assertive is a problem for you, remember that three "what the heck" meals can be 1,200 to 1,800 high-fat calories each, compared with the 600 sensible calories that you probably would consume at home. This adds up to at least a half-pound of body fat. How often do you dine out?

Planning Your Strategy

- Plan ahead by eating a small appetite-dulling snack before dinner. Raw vegetables, "Miracle Soup" (see my recipe on page 154) or a piece of fruit are good choices. You will avoid a feeding frenzy at the restaurant.
- Call ahead to ask about the menu and request help if necessary.
- Decide in advance what you want to order or scan the menu as soon as it comes. If it does not appear to be rude, volunteer to order first. You will set the tone for the meal. Should dissenters try to sway you, it's too late, as you have already ordered.
- If you dine out frequently you may want to stick with a few favourite restaurants. As the servers get to know you they will anticipate your requests.
- Always ask how dishes are prepared.
- Take clear soups or tomato-based soups over chowders or creamed soups. Ask if puréed soups contain cream.
- Look for appetizers with vegetables, fish or pasta. Avoid fried and saucy dishes.
- Beware of the salad bar. Potato salad and coleslaw can be loaded with mayonnaise. Other salads, like marinated vegetables and pasta salads, are full of oil. If you do visit the salad bar, choose fresh vegetables and put a little dressing on the side of your plate.
- Remember that Caesar, Greek and julienne salads with dressing are high-fat choices.
- Marinated dishes, like antipasto salads, are soaked in oil.
- Avoid pan-fried, deep-fried, stir-fried, crisp, battered and breaded, sautéed, basted and tempura.
- Choose poached, steamed, grilled, broiled without butter, charbroiled, barbecued, baked, roasted and boiled.
- Avoid Hollandaise, Béarnaise, Alfredo, white sauce, cheese sauce, *au fromage*, butter sauce, lemon butter, cream sauce and gravies.
- Choose tomato sauce, tomato or other broth, marinara, in white wine, *au naturel* and seafood sauce.
- Minimize red meat consumption and look for a leaner cut *au jus* (prepared in its own juice) rather than a fatty cut such as prime rib. You'll be surprised at the flavour this style of cooking adds.

PHOTO: Cinnamon and Vanilla Glazed French Toast (page 142); Apple Flan (page 146)

- Avoid scalloped and *au gratin*. There are lots of low-cal toppings for baked potatoes — fresh dill, parsley or chives with no-fat yogurt. Cottage cheese, salsa, Dijon mustard or low-fat tzatziki are also great.
- Onion rings are deep-fried just like french fries.
- Avoid dishes in fatty pastry shells — for example quiche and meat pies — and stay clear of casseroles, as they frequently contain cream sauce.
- If the entrees are not appropriate, consider two appetizers and a large salad with dressing on the side.
- If you are very hungry, order a side dish of vegetables, steamed or grilled without butter or oil. Drizzle a bit of salad dressing on them for added flavour.
- If the portion you receive is too large for you, give some to another person at the table, or immediately request a doggie bag. (Ask that it be kept in the refrigerator for you until the end of the meal.) If you can't do either, pour salt or pepper liberally on part of the meal, so you won't eat it inadvertently while engrossed in conversation or by taking "just one more bite." And don't feel guilty about wasting the food, as in this situation it would otherwise wind up around your middle.
- You don't want to wear chocolate cake, either, long after the taste has worn away. If you want dessert, order fresh fruit or an ice. However, eating fruit immediately after a meal will bloat some people. Cappuccino with a little sweetener is a rich-tasting substitute for dessert. If you are comfortably full, consider whether your desire for dessert is simply an automatic response.
- If the neighbourhood is safe, a leisurely walk back to the car will help you digest your meal.

BEST BETS FOR FAST FOOD

Our demands used to be for cheap and fast food. Fast-food restaurants are now also becoming more aware of health. But, in spite of the healthier choices recently introduced, they still have a long way to go. Traditional fast foods are high in fat, sugar and sodium and low in fibre. However, many new "healthier" choices are not as great as they are made out to be. Occasional fast-food meals are

PHOTO: *Steamed Artichoke with Tzatziki Dip (page 151);*
Carrot Ginger Soup (page 154)

okay as long as they don't become a regular part of your diet. Let's look at the best and worst choices.

- Stick with a small, regular-sized hamburger, and avoid the larger choices. Remember that regular-sized, plain fast food hamburgers provide about 75% of their calories from fat. Sometimes low-fat hamburgers are also available. But when these are advertised as 28% of calories from fat, we are not told that the bun is considered in the calculation. The patty still provides 50% of its calories from fat! Load up on lettuce and tomatoes and minimize pickles, which are high in salt. Better yet, round out the meal with a salad. In many restaurants you can even get low-cal salad dressing.
- Avoid hot dogs at all costs. They are high in fat and often contain questionable ingredients.
- Broiled chicken breast on a bun is good. Avoid breaded chicken or chicken fingers, which are deep-fried in unhealthy oils and contain fatty skin. Fried and breaded fish sandwiches are also high in fat.
- Low-fat ice cream and frozen yogurt (used in shakes and cones) are low in fat but substantially higher in sugar than regular varieties. One shake contains as much as 11 teaspoons of sugar. So they are only slightly lower in calories than regular varieties.
- Choose baked potatoes instead of fries and go easy on the butter.
- Cereal is now available for breakfast at some fast-food outlets. Scrambled eggs (if they are not cooked in butter or oil) on an English muffin are a good alternative. Some places will make omelettes or scrambled eggs with three egg whites and only one yolk. It can't hurt to ask. And some also serve low-fat ham. Avoid cheese, bacon, sausages and croissants, as these are mainly fat.

INTERNATIONAL FOODS

Chinese

I hate to break the news to you, but Chinese food can be the worst choice you'll ever make. However, I know that most of you don't want to give it up, so consider these easy-to-follow guidelines.

Soy sauce and MSG are the most common flavourings used in Chinese food. And fat hides everywhere, not just in the obviously fried foods, such as egg rolls and spring rolls, which are almost all fat. Stir-fries use lots of oil, and the meat or fish portions are frequently deep fried before being added to the dish so they will not fall apart when tossed around in the wok. Steamed dim sum dishes also contain seafood and meats that have been fried first. Even lobster and fish often are fried unless you ask for them to be prepared in another way.

Ask for no MSG and use soy sauce sparingly. Clear soups are good alternatives, although they may contain MSG. Any steamed dish, such as steamed shrimp or steamed chicken and vegetables, is a great substitute to a stir-fry. You can then add seasonings such as soy, hot mustard or sweet-and-sour sauce in small quantities.

Mexican
Mexican food is a nightmare of fat. Beef tacos and enchiladas, chili, cheese, avocadoes, sour cream and corn chips are full of fat. And refried beans are just that — fried twice in oil.

Choose chicken fajitas and load up on lettuce, tomato and salsa, avoiding the cheese, avocado and sour cream that normally accompany this dish.

Japanese
Sushi, noriwraps, miso soup, teriyaki chicken and fish, and seaweed salads are all good choices. Avoid tempura, as it is fried.

Southern and "Island" Chicken
Traditionally prepared chicken is fried, or breaded and then fried, but there are several places to get baked and rotisserie chicken. Try not to eat the skin, which is all fat. Also, note that white meat is lower in fat than dark meat.

Delicatessen
Smoked meats and salami are very high in sodium and fat, although many delis are beginning to carry low-fat meats, such as low-fat ham. When such substitutions are not available, turkey and chicken sandwiches are good low-fat alternatives. Some delis also use

low-fat mayonnaise in their tuna, egg and salmon salads, and often coho salmon is used, which is leaner than sockeye. Always ask. Avoid white bread and choose rye, whole wheat or pumpernickel.

Pickles and olives are full of salt, and olives are high in fat. You are already aware of the dangers of french fries, potato salad, cakes, coffee and soft drinks. Now, does deli food still appeal to you?

Pizza

The danger of pizza is in high-fat, high-sodium toppings such as pepperoni, sausage, prosciutto, extra cheese, olives and anchovies. Many crusts are high in oil. Lower-fat frozen pizzas are now available — check for them in health food stores and read labels to find the sodium content.

Many gourmet pizza outlets offer some great alternatives — thin crusts, low-fat mozzarella and a large variety of vegetable toppings.

EATING AT PARTIES

There's no doubt about it, a cold beer or a glass of fine wine with some of those little appetizer-size hot dogs or phyllo pastry snacks help make a party great. But at 100 calories plus per drink and 100 to 200 calories per pop for finger foods, 2,000 calories can go by quickly. If you drink regularly — two beers, two glasses of wine, or 2 ounces of hard liquor a day — that's about 1,500 calories per week, or more than 75,000 calories in a year: enough calories to create and maintain 21 pounds of extra fat. Also, while food contains important nutrients, alcohol doesn't. The key to weight maintenance is to consume nutrient-dense foods and to avoid or minimize those empty calorie choices. As well, excessive alcohol consumption uses up vitamins B and C and leaches calcium out of your system when it's metabolized.

You don't have to avoid parties to stay healthy. Here are some alternatives to caloric suicide. As with restaurant eating, don't arrive starving. When you start to drink on an empty stomach, your will-power shuts down quickly, which often leads to an uncontrollable pig-out. Avoid fattening or salted foods — salted foods are usually fattening as well, and increase your thirst. Some of my clients like to park themselves by the raw veggies and fill up on them and a few shrimp before circulating around the room. If plates are available for snack foods, take a *small* one.

If you are going to drink hard liquor, choose lower-proof alcohols; 100-proof liquor has 10 more calories per ounce than does 90-proof. Adding 8 ounces tonic water, cola or ginger ale to liquor adds 120 calories of sugar. Use a diet mix and alternate between drinking water and alcoholic beverages. You will reduce your caloric intake by 75%.

Another problem that alcohol causes for those trying to lose weight is that, since it is absorbed quickly into the blood, blood sugar rises rapidly. To compensate, insulin is secreted, and insulin is a fat-hoarding hormone. It makes less fat available for the body's energy needs.

Good alternatives to booze are soda or mineral waters with a twist, diet cola with lime, or a Virgin Mary. Some non-alcoholic beer and wine tastes pretty good, as well. To reduce the effects of a hangover, make sure when drinking alcohol to alternate it with plenty of non-alcoholic beverages. In fact, it's best to have one glass of water or equivalent for every alcoholic drink consumed, as a hangover is largely a state of dehydration. If your friends pressure you to drink, plan an excuse ahead of time, for example appoint yourself designated driver. When all else fails, I say that I'm taking antibiotics.

If you're the one throwing the party, make diet drinks available; buy low-fat crackers and snack food; use no-fat yogurt instead of sour cream and mayonnaise when you mix the dips, and try honey mustard, Dijon, salsa and veggie dips. (See pages 148 to 151 for veggie dips.) Make a pizza with a thin crust, low-fat cheese and grilled vegetables. Crystal Light is a great base for a low-cal punch, or try President's Choice low-calorie Pink Grapefruit, Cranberry or Cranberry/Raspberry juices.

SET MEALS

The toughest meals to cope with are those served at other people's homes. Aside from sneaking what you don't want to the dog, you're stuck. If you can, speak with your host or hostess about your eating habits ahead of time, so that there will be some healthy choices available. If you're in a bind, make sure to eat a small snack before the event. Then search out the least damaging choices during the meal, avoid or scrape off any excess sauce or gravy, take small servings and consider going home a little hungry.

Catered functions, on the other hand, are a snap to deal with. Simply call the hotel, restaurant or banquet hall ahead of time. Ask for the catering department, state politely that your doctor has you on a low-fat, low-cholesterol diet and discuss the menu. My clients and I have never encountered problems obtaining an alternative meal. (Caterers frequently receive requests for vegetarian, kosher and other special meals.) Don't forget at the end of the conversation to ask for the full name of the person with whom you are speaking, as this will help to ensure the person's cooperation.

When you arrive at the function, tell the maître d' that you have ordered a special meal and where you will be sitting. Or, when you sit down you can quietly notify your server of your arranged meal. Some of you may consider this process rude. However, caterers can easily make substitutions, and the more requests they receive the sooner they will realize that good-tasting food also can be healthy food. I have developed enough alternative menus for exclusive hotels and spas to know that *healthy* and *gourmet* are not mutually exclusive terms.

HOLIDAY EATING

Holidays are often the time our will-power is most adversely affected. It seems that one mistake leads to the attitude, "What the heck, I've blown it already, so I might as well go for it." The most important thing to realize here is that one mistake, or one high-calorie evening, won't cause a problem. It's the next 2,000 or 3,000 fat-filled calories that do the damage. The weight goes on in a couple of days and takes weeks to lose.

During holidays use the suggestions I have already given you, and realize that planning is important. As with the rest of life, if you think ahead, the pieces fall into place much more easily. Decide what you will eat and leave time for physical activities to help burn off the extra calories. Doing something active with family or friends can be just as much fun as eating.

If snacking is a problem, try not to participate in kitchen-centred activities like cooking or cleaning up. Instead, help in other ways. If your responsibilities at this time are demanding, make some time to relax so that you will not eat to relieve your stress. Your holiday time should be more rewarding then ever before, and so should the time immediately after the holiday, as you will feel refreshed — and not like a guilt-ridden slug.

EATING ON AIRPLANES

Almost all airlines offer a variety of special meals. These range from low-fat to low-calorie, low-salt, kosher, vegetarian and seafood. They often taste better than standard fare. Special meals without MSG help minimize the bloated feeling that some of us are left with after flying. Advise your travel agent to arrange meals for you, or call the airline at least 48 hours ahead of your flight. When you confirm your return flight confirm the meal you ordered. I also like to take a bag of cut-up vegetables with me. They're great to snack on and round out airplane meals.

Minimize jet lag:
- Eat a high carbohydrate meal before and during the flight. This will help minimize dehydration. Drink adequate fluids with your meals. And try to drink 8 ounces of fluid per hour during the flight.
- Avoid excess coffee, tea, alcohol and caffeinated soft drinks, which are dehydrating.
- Move around the plane every so often and stretch as best you can. This prevents stiffness and fatigue. Also try to rest or sleep during part of the flight — meditation is great.
- When you arrive at your destination, if possible, try to get outside into the light; don't confine yourself to the indoors.
- Adopt your arrival time early. If you arrive in the morning try to take only a short nap. Setting your watch to the destination time before takeoff helps to trick your body into following the new time.

Chapter 13
EXERCISE IS EASY

THE MORE YOU EXERCISE — UP TO A POINT — THE LONGER YOU ARE likely to live. Those going from low to moderate fitness levels show the biggest health improvements, although the fittest people are usually the healthiest overall. "Fittest," however, does not mean those who exercise the most or the most intensely — it means those who exercise appropriately to get into the best cardiovascular shape possible. But even people who do their own yard work and heavy housework, take regular walks, use the stairs more frequently and so on will benefit from their efforts.

THE BENEFITS OF EXERCISE

I love to exercise. It makes me feel great, helps me maintain my weight, gives me lots of strength and energy and helps me to sleep well at night. It keeps my blood pressure and cholesterol normal, strengthens my heart and lungs and boosts my immune system in its fight against illness and disease. It improves my frustration tolerance and is a great alternative to eating as a way to release stress. Exercise also reduces nervousness and relieves depression and irritability. When my clients lose weight through a combination of diet and exercise, their self-esteem and sense of accomplishment improve noticeably.

There are several reasons exercise keeps us feeling young. We don't feel old because we are old — we feel old as we age because we adopt sedentary lifestyles that accelerate the deterioration of our bodies. Muscle decreases and is replaced with fat. Our hearts can't pump as much blood. Our arteries clog and our blood pressure rises. Joints stiffen and our energy levels drop.

To a large extent, no matter how old we are, exercise can reverse these changes. And exercise is particularly helpful in protecting against the slow but steady weight gain that we experience as we grow older. The vast majority of people of all ages who are able to achieve and maintain a healthy weight participate in regular aerobic exercise. Almost all of us can exercise if we are properly instructed, no matter how old we are, even if we are injured or invalid. People with physical restrictions should consult a sports therapist or a physiotherapist who can create a customized exercise program.

WHAT QUALIFIES AS EXERCISE? YOU MAY BE SURPRISED!

Our ancestors led very physical lives. So, as a population, they never had to worry about getting enough exercise. Pen-pushing and sedentary jobs have been around in large numbers for only the past two generations. Most of us also have convenient transportation at our disposal, so we don't walk or bicycle as frequently as we should.

When you get the urge to exercise, do you lie down until it goes away? Or get a cold beer and do some serious bicep curls? Take it from me, exercise can be fun. And once you begin to reap the benefits, you'll enjoy it so much that you will wonder why you avoided it for so long. If you can't bring yourself to participate in vigorous exercise, try to put in 45 to 60 minutes doing an enjoyable activity five or six days a week. Dancing, baseball, gardening and washing the car all qualify. Whatever your chosen activity, do it at a moderate, constant pace. You'll soon notice how good you feel.

I'm going to focus on the role of aerobic fitness, because it's most important to cardiovascular health and fat burning. But remember, overall fitness is a combination of cardiovascular endurance, muscular strength, muscular endurance and flexibility. Exercises that build muscular strength and endurance also tone you; they get rid of unwanted flab and help to minimize back problems. However, to be truly fit and to minimize your chance of injury, you should develop all four elements, not just one or two.

A minimum of 30 minutes of moderate, continuous and consistent aerobic exercise, four to five times each week, is best for the combined goals of weight loss, fat burning and aerobic health. Exercising less frequently is not as effective for fat burning. But don't overdo it! Those who exercise six times or more a week suffer more overuse injuries than people who exercise four or five times. It is also essential that you slowly increase the frequency and duration of your exercise. Overtraining — too much exercise for your current state of fitness — produces uncomfortable side effects and increases the risk of injury.

To minimize overfatigue and possible injury of specific muscles, try cross training. Cross training normally consists of regular participation in two or three aerobic exercises, for example walking, cycling and rowing. I suggest, once or twice a week, continuous participation in two or three chosen exercises *during the same session*. The reason is simple.

If you tire after 20 to 30 minutes of walking — a lower body exercise — fat burning will decrease. By switching to rowing, which is primarily an upper body exercise, you will have enough glycogen (energy) in your upper body to keep exercising aerobically for another 20 to 30 minutes. Ideally a 20/20/20 combination of cross training is best, switching from lower body to upper body, then to lower body or whole body exercise.

Rowing and jogging, rowing and walking, and rowing and bicycling are good combinations. For workouts that use the entire body, try cross country skiing, circuit training with weights (low to medium resistance and a higher number of repetitions, when you do not have to wait to use equipment), or go to classes in low- or high-impact or step aerobics. Adding variety to your workouts keeps you motivated. Remember, any exercise that is part of a fat-burning routine must be done consistently, continuously and with medium intensity.

Although it uses all major muscles and is very easy on joints, swimming is not a fat-burning activity, because to stay warm in the water, the body minimizes fat mobilization. However, water walking and aquabics, while still burning less fat, can be effective alternatives to walking and swimming.

EXERCISE AND HYDRATION

Remember to drink plenty of fluid before and after exercise. Restricting fluid intake can reduce strength, endurance and overall athletic performance. You must make an effort to drink because your thirst is usually satisfied long before you have replenished lost fluids. Cool water (40 to 50°F) is the best choice because it is most readily absorbed by the stomach. If the air is hot or if you exercise for more than one hour, it's a good idea to drink *during* exercise, as well.

In hot weather consume 16 to 20 ounces of water two hours before you exercise, another 8 ounces 15 to 30 minutes before, and 4 to 8 ounces every 10 to 20 minutes during exercise. Also, drink after you have exercised. If you want to take a technical approach, weigh yourself before and after a demanding workout. For every pound of weight you lose, drink 16 ounces of water. In cool weather you may be able to halve consumption, as dehydration and heat exhaustion are not as great a concern. However, if you perspire about the same amount, drink the same amount as you would in the heat.

And speaking of heat, don't underestimate the potential for heat exhaustion when exercising aerobically outdoors in very warm weather. It's easy to overdo it, particularly when you are not acclimatized. Similarly, when travelling, don't try to keep up with the locals. In a hot climate, exercise in early morning or late in the day.

Through repeated workouts in warm weather your body will learn to conserve salt and will adjust to the heat. If you perspire profusely, a good post-exercise recovery meal will replace lost salt. And both before and after your workout, eat foods such as bananas and oranges, which are high in potassium, an essential mineral.

The use of sports drinks to provide sugar, potassium and other minerals is growing rapidly, thanks to the major advertising investments made by manufacturers. As a general guide, unless you are exercising intensely for more than one hour, these drinks don't seem to provide advantages over water. Water replacement is the most important goal when exercising moderately. Additionally, the sugar content of these drinks varies widely. The more sugary drinks may be absorbed too slowly for adequate hydration, and may make you nauseated. Sometimes a sports drink will work better for you when it's diluted. The coaches I have consulted with agree that experimentation and reviewing new research are the only ways to find the best sports drink for yourself. However, studies continue to show that water, fruit and other wholesome carbohydrates do the best job.

Whatever you do, don't go for that cold beer until after you have cooled down, showered and had some water. All alcohol is dehydrating. And finally, although some people like to sweat, never dress too warmly. It won't help you to lose weight, but will dehydrate you and possibly lead to heatstroke.

THE DO'S AND DON'TS OF EXERCISE

Exercise is the most inconsistently and improperly practised preventive health measure. Many people do more damage to themselves by exercising than they would do by abstaining. They run excessive distances; they wear improper shoes and run on hard pavement; they bicycle in gears that are too high. They recklessly lift barbells and weights that are far too heavy for them. These errors ruin their ankles, knees and backs. People don't stretch at all or they stretch improperly, causing their muscles and ligaments to tighten up or to be strained unnecessarily. Perhaps worst of all, they alternate between compulsive, high-intensity aerobic exercise and a couch potato lifestyle. Their cardiovascular systems are shocked by overuse then underuse.

We have to learn to exercise regularly and responsibly. The goal is to improve our cardiovascular function, our strength, flexibility and endurance, to burn excess calories — and to have fun. I want to emphasize some important points that many of us forget.

Before you begin a program of safe exercise, you should have a physical exam, including a cardiovascular stress test. The best exercise program to start with is one that you can comfortably stick to. Setting excessively high goals only increases your chance of injury and reduces the likelihood of maintaining the regimen. And a routine that is too easy will not meet the requirements for aerobic fitness or fat burning.

The first step to developing a successful program is to forget the slogan "no pain, no gain." Pain is often an early warning sign of injury. However, when you start to exercise, you may be stiff and sore afterward, as your muscles are not used to the increased work load. Stretching, massage and hot baths or Jacuzzis are great. Persistence is necessary. The stiffness will go away after the first week or so.

Exercising should be fun, so choose activities you enjoy. This will help overcome your reluctance and fears. With a qualified fitness instructor, write down a list of realistic goals, and learn how to record your progress. The goal of any aerobic exercise is to raise your heart rate and maintain it in its training range — the number of beats per minute that is proper for you. You may find this type of exertion uncomfortable at first. Give yourself a chance to become used to it.

WALKING FOR HEALTH

Walking is the cheapest, easiest and most versatile aerobic exercise there is. All you need are a pair of good shoes and some interesting routes. It is also easier on your back, knees and other joints than jogging. Since exercise for purposes of fat burning should not be too intense, brisk walking is often the ideal choice to begin with.

Don't forget to warm up before you walk and to cool down and stretch after you walk. Stretching to your favourite music is relaxing. Learn how to stretch properly, to prevent tearing tissue.

Walking briskly with a companion is, besides a social activity, probably the best aerobic start for anyone who is overweight and underexercised. If you want to start walking, unless you are quite overweight or have never exercised, start with a 1- to 2-mile walk. Go as far and as fast as you comfortably can. Don't push yourself and don't time yourself. A competitive attitude will work against you. Slow down if you become winded or can't speak without panting for air.

Do this four or five times per week, and try to go a little farther each time, until you can keep at it for 30 minutes. Then try to increase your speed. Work up to a 3.5 to 4 mph pace if you are a woman of average height, and 4.5 to 5 mph if you are a man of average height. If you can't walk quickly, try to walk for a longer period. As you improve, increase the time of your walks to 40 to 60 minutes. Start swinging your arms to increase the aerobic benefit. Carrying a 5- to 10-pound backpack will have the same effect.

Once you are in shape, tailor your routine by letting your feelings be your guide to the amount and duration of exercise you do each day. During busy times, you can maintain your level of conditioning by working out for 30 to 45 minutes only three times a week.

If you have not exercised for a long time, don't be impatient. Give yourself at least one month to notice the benefits. Then you can begin to record your progress and work toward your goals. Monitoring your heart rate will help you to derive the maximum benefit from your exercise while avoiding overexertion.

VARIETY IS A KEY TO MOTIVATION

Exercise should never become boring or painful. As you reach your aerobic goals, raise them accordingly. Keep a written record. It will keep you on track, let you set realistic challenges, build confidence and minimize frustration. When you have a good base, should you want to you can also start more vigorous activities, like aerobic classes. Varying your exercise routine is a great way to keep your interest piqued, to work on your weakest link and to minimize the chance of overuse injuries.

Exercising with friends can provide motivation and relieve boredom. To add variety, you can alternate the friends you work out with, exercise out of doors or vary your walking route and incorporate some hills for additional challenge. When you travel, walking or cycling is a great way to see things you would otherwise miss. And you can discover many new parts of your own city this way, too. Brisk walking burns 300 calories or more per hour. Even slow walking uses 120 to 150 calories an hour!

There are lots of ways to fit walking and bicycling into your routine:

- Get off the bus or subway a few stops earlier and walk the rest of the way.
- Walk or bicycle to the grocery store.
- Buy a treadmill or stationary bicycle and use it while reading or watching television. To avoid boredom, tape shows and fast forward through the commercials.
- Put a kiddy seat on the bicycle and take a trip with your child.
- If it's too hot or cold outside, walk in the local mall; or climb the stairs at the office or in your (or a friend's) apartment building. Generally, don't avoid the stairs — begin to appreciate what they can do for you
- Go dancing, or sign up for lessons.

Part III
THE 24 QUESTIONS MY CLIENTS MOST FREQUENTLY ASK

1. Why is it that every time I go on a diet it becomes increasingly difficult to lose weight?

The weight you lose on a diet is not weight you can keep off. On the contrary, yo-yo dieting, or on-again, off-again dieting, can make you fat. It's also hazardous to your health, and leaves your skin flabby.

After you lose weight and return to your old way of eating, your caloric consumption and fat intake increase rapidly. Usually they go back to their original levels, and the weight returns. Weight loss becomes increasingly difficult with each subsequent effort for two reasons. The first problem is that when you diet to lose weight you can lose a lot of lean muscle tissue along with the fat. This situation is most common when you eat less than 1,200 calories per day, or when you eat an unbalanced diet. The more rapid the weight loss, the higher the ratio of lean muscle tissue to fat that is lost. The second cruel truth is that as you regain weight after the diet is over, fat returns, but lean muscle tissue does not. Remember, fat cells don't disappear. They merely shrink, then wait for a doughnut or french fries to fill them again. And your body learns to store the fat you eat more quickly and efficiently after each dieting effort.

Here's an example. When you quickly lose 20 pounds, 10 of these pounds are fat, 6 pounds are water and 4 pounds are muscle tissue. When the 20 pounds that you lose so quickly in a crash diet are regained, you gain 12 pounds of fat, 8 pounds of water and —unless you exercise vigorously — none of it is lean muscle. As the yo-yo dieting cycle continues, the fat-to-muscle ratio continues to rise.

Lean muscle is more metabolically active than fat — it requires more calories to sustain itself. After you have crept back up to your old weight, with a higher fat-to-lean-muscle ratio, you won't require as many calories as you did before the diet to maintain that weight. It will also become increasingly difficult to lose the regained weight. To diet again, you must consume even fewer calories each day than you did while on the first diet. The result is that you can gain the weight back twice as fast, but it can take almost twice as long to lose it the second time around!

Fad diets can promise rapid weight loss in the first two weeks, but you are losing water and lean muscle tissue. Diet pills don't work, either. They can have horrible side effects and are dangerous to your health. Whatever the diet plan, the instructions always forget to tell you that whatever you did to take the weight off, you must do for the rest of your life if you don't want to gain the weight back. If they told us the truth, we wouldn't buy into the diet in the first place.

If this information makes you angry — and I hope it does — use the energy in a new way. Go for a run; throw out a bag of cookies. Best of all, adopt a healthy nutritional lifestyle. If you need to lose weight, do it slowly — 1 to 2 pounds per week. Eat sensibly, drink plenty of water and exercise to help keep the weight off. You didn't get heavy overnight, so why must you lose the weight so quickly?

2. Why is it that when my husband and I diet together he always loses weight twice as fast as I do?

Diets typically limit you to 1,200 to 1,500 calories per day. If you and your husband go on the same diet, his caloric deficit will be higher than yours and he will lose weight faster for two reasons. First, if he is heavier than you, his caloric demand will still be proportionately higher than yours. Every pound of body weight requires a certain number of calories each day to maintain itself. If, for example, your husband weighs 250 pounds and you weigh 150, the calories that he eats every day must be sufficient to support an extra 100 pounds. When he starts eating less, his caloric deficit will be proportionately greater and have a bigger effect on his weight loss.

Secondly, men have more muscle than women. Although women can develop tremendous definition through exercise, to meet the needs of reproduction they have a greater percentage of body fat than men. Lean muscle tissue is more metabolically active than fat, so men at rest burn more calories than women at rest. Again, he is eating about as much as you are, but burning more calories than you just to maintain his muscle mass.

You and your husband should not consume the same number of calories when trying to lose weight. Simply eat healthfully while slightly restricting your caloric intake, and you should both lose a maximum of 2 pounds a week.

3. Is it more difficult to lose weight as I age?

If we keep active, the rate at which we burn calories decreases by 1 to 2% each decade. If our lifestyle becomes substantially more sedentary as we age, it can slow up to 10%. Often, the older we get, the lazier we become. We park closer to the entrance of the mall, we exercise less and we don't play with the children (as they are no longer children). These changes can dramatically reduce our daily caloric expenditure.

If we don't exercise as we age, our muscle mass declines with disuse. This change further reduces our caloric needs. But we rarely change our eating behaviour to compensate for reduced caloric need. On the contrary, we frequently lounge around and snack more often. Burning 100 fewer calories per day without decreasing our total caloric consumption can mean a gain of 5 or more pounds per year. Start snacking, and you can easily put on 10 to 15 pounds in a year!

4. Is fasting a good way to lose weight?

As a way to lose weight, fasting is definitely not acceptable. There are no advantages to fasting except perhaps for those who are grossly overweight and under a doctor's care. When you stop eating there is a rapid initial weight loss, but most of it is fluid rather than fat. Besides, as soon as you have a meal, you may gain a substantial amount of weight back.

To compensate for the reduced intake of fuel, your body slows its metabolic rate. When our metabolism slows, we don't burn fat as quickly. And when we later increase our caloric consumption, we store the calories as fat much more easily.

In addition, our bodies need some protein each day. Without it they break down muscle tissue (which is made of protein) to

provide the fuel for cell regeneration and other essential processes. Loss of muscle tissue can account for up to 30% of any rapid
weight loss. Reduced muscle tissue further lowers your metabolic rate. (See question 1.) In the end you will have more fat, less
muscle and a slower metabolism. Few people who lose weight this
way maintain their loss, and some develop gall stones or sustain
permanent injury. Sensible eating and regular aerobic and mus-
cle-toning exercise will get you back on track.

Finally, consider that fasting and other radical forms of dieting
require that you deny yourself everything you like. In such a state,
food is all you will think about, and when the fast ends, you will
have some serious making up to do, thereby defeating the purpose
of the fast. The key to sensible eating is not to make major sacrifices. Learning to choose appropriate alternatives is easy.

5. Can a high-protein diet help me to retain lean muscle while losing fat?

We require only a moderate amount of protein to maintain lean
muscle mass while losing weight. Eating a high-protein diet without carbohydrates leads to excessive fluid loss. The best way to
build and maintain muscle mass while dieting is to train with light
weights and eat a balanced diet.

Most people need about 45 to 55 grams of protein a day to prevent muscle tissue loss. There are about 21 grams of protein in 3
ounces of cooked, lean meat, fish or fowl (without skin). An 8-
ounce glass of low-fat milk has 8 grams, as does a half cup of lentils.
Four ounces of tofu can pack a whopping 14 grams! By eating small
amounts of animal protein and focusing on grains, legumes and
vegetables, you will consume ample protein.

6. Does it matter what time of day I eat my meals? Can I save most of my calories for dinner?

Some people are not hungry in the morning and prefer to eat
later. Breakfast is not a must, and a piece of fruit or toast may be
enough. Others may prefer to eat mid-morning, which is also fine
if they don't get symptoms of low blood sugar.

However, eating nothing all morning and then having a large
lunch rich in carbohydrates can cause extreme fatigue shortly

thereafter. A large meal diverts blood into the stomach for digestion, and this contributes to lethargy. Large carbohydrate meals also cause the secretion of hormones that calm and relax. The effect is called "postprandial depression." In addition, our bodies are naturally inclined to feel sleepy sometime in the afternoon. If this time coincides with the time we are digesting a large lunch, we feel even more sleepy.

You should eat lunch, especially if you have not had breakfast. If you are frequently tired after lunch, watch the quantity that you eat; go for a moderate amount of carbohydrate and mainly low-fat protein (which enhances the secretion of chemicals that contribute to alertness).

If you don't eat all day, there's no fuel in the tank to run your engine. You won't feel as good as you could. Frequently you will be so hungry at dinner that you end up overeating. Evening is most people's least active time of day. When you are inactive, calories burn more slowly and are stored as fat more readily. If you don't eat all day your metabolism is even slower in the evening, contributing to even more fat storage. Carbohydrates eaten late in the day help relax some people. If you need energy, proteins may help to pick you up.

If you are not particularly hungry in the morning and eat a small lunch but want to control yourself at dinner, try eating four to six healthy snack-type meals each day. Try a piece of fruit or toast in the morning; fruit, a bagel or a small bowl of cereal mid-morning; a small lunch; cut-up vegetables or soup in the afternoon; a small dinner; and fruit or cereal in the evening.

7. *What is my ideal weight?*

It depends on whom you ask. Standard weight tables, developed by the insurance industry, do not consider race, age and other variables. The use of callipers to measure body fat can be inaccurate and inconsistent, as different technicians will not necessarily position the calliper at the same place. Another common way to decide how much you should weigh is to use the Body Mass Index (BMI), which plugs height and weight into a simple formula.

There is no universally accepted method by which to measure ideal weight or obesity. The terms "overweight" and "obese" are frequently used interchangeably, but they do not mean the same thing. Current North American thinking concludes that the BMI is the most reasonable guideline for defining "overweight," because here "overweight" is the weight at which we become significantly at risk to endangering our health. Those who exceed their ideal or desirable weight by 20% or more, according to this measure, are overweight.

This solution is an intelligent one. But the problem with it, or any definition of obesity or ideal weight, is that not only are we measuring by a less than perfect method but we are also trying to apply some standard measure to a huge variety of body types. For example, some people have a heavier musculature than others, with thick muscular legs and a dense, heavy skeleton. Their BMI may be higher than acceptable, but they won't necessarily have higher health risks. A slim male who carries all of his fat around his middle might have a safe BMI (although his weight would not be acceptable by calliper measure), but he is at risk because of the location of his fat. A fat middle is clearly connected to higher incidence of heart disease in men.

My experience has led me to use the following guideline as the best general approach to ideal weight. Compare the results you get using it to the BMI chart on the opposite page. Note that the system I use applies to all adults over 5 feet tall, except pregnant women and those over 65. (BMI has even more exceptions than these groups.)

Small Frame

A small frame is determined by slim wrists and ankles and narrow hips and/or shoulders.

Ideal weight for women with a small frame is 100 pounds at 5 feet, plus 5 pounds for each additional inch of height. A woman who is 5 foot 6 would thus ideally weigh 100 + (5 x 6), or 130 pounds.

Ideal weight for men with a small frame is 110 pounds at 5 feet, plus 6 pounds for each additional inch. A 6-foot man would thus ideally weigh 110 + (6 x 12), or 182 pounds.

SIZE UP YOUR WEIGHT

Health experts use a scientific measure called the Body Mass Index (BMI) to figure out whether your weight is healthy. To make it easy, here's a chart that will show your BMI in four easy steps.

• Mark an X at your height on Scale A.
• Mark an X at your weight on Scale B.
• Draw a line to join the two X's.
• Extend this line to Scale C.
Where the line meets Scale C is your BMI.

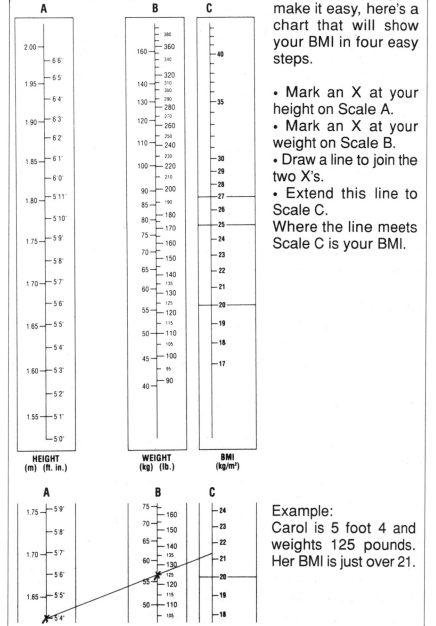

Example:
Carol is 5 foot 4 and weights 125 pounds. Her BMI is just over 21.

Adapted by the Ontario Ministry of Health from charts produced by Health and Welfare Canada

Medium Frame

If you have a medium frame, add 5 pounds to the ideal weight figure.

Large Frame

If you have a large frame — thick wrists and ankles, broad hips and/or shoulders — add 10 pounds to the ideal weight figure.

Above all, realize that your body shape can make a difference to your ideal weight. Obviously, the closer you come to overweight as defined by any measure, the greater your health risks may be, and on a day-to-day level you probably won't feel as good as you otherwise could.

Don't become obsessed with any one method of finding exactly how much you should weigh. Likewise, don't simply use the method that gives you the most favourable results. If you think that your weight is not healthy, review your eating behaviour and consider consulting a nutritionist. If you still feel you need to lose some weight when others insist that you are slim, see the answer to the next question.

The Big Exceptions

The BMI is designed for adults aged 20 to 65 years — those whose body size and composition are fairly stable.

It does not apply to babies, children, adolescents, pregnant or nursing women, senior citizens, *very* muscular people, and endurance athletes such as runners.

8. *I can't seem to keep off those last 5 pounds. What should I do?*

Let's face it, the only thing a lot of us think about as much as sex is weight loss. We're led to believe that the ideal body type is lean and trim. (If you're a man, add some rippling muscle.) Such images lead almost 90% of North Americans to think that they are at least 5 pounds overweight. Many of us could stand to lose some weight, and about 40% of us are following some weight-loss program at any given time. However, studies show that only between 15 and 25% of us are truly obese. The final analysis is that the advertising industry has totally brainwashed us — if we don't look like the people in fashion ads, we're losers. As a result, many people aspire to maintain a weight that is 5 pounds less than what is optimal for their body type, and are therefore almost constantly on a diet. If they settled for being just 5 pounds heavier, they could eat in a more natural and healthy way, without the constant guilt.

We must accept the fact that we don't have to be pencil thin and we should not sacrifice our nutrition and health for the sake of being skinny. If your perceived ideal weight is difficult to maintain, it is too low. Yo-yoing up and down 5 pounds does more damage than if your weight is stable.

Furthermore, after losing weight, the body takes about six months to adjust to the new lower weight. This is the most critical time during which to ensure that weight loss is permanent. Instead of trying to drop that last 5 pounds, focus on doing the right things to maintain your new weight. This will help your body to adjust to the new weight as your new "set point." (A set point is a weight at which the body feels comfortable, often a healthy weight that you maintained when younger.) It is possible to change your set point with continued adherence to calorie restriction and regular exercise. But give yourself a chance to stabilize at your new weight first.

During extensive weight loss, you may reach two or three plateaus — weights that you stick at for some time — as you hit old set points. The first plateau can come after an initial week or two of caloric restriction, because at this point you no longer lose water weight. (Water comes off the fastest.)

If you have started to exercise, you may even gain some weight as you develop new muscle. If you exercise regularly, when you finish your diet you may be 5 or so pounds heavier than you want to be because you are more muscular than before. Remember, muscle weighs more than fat, but it looks better, too. Finally, to maximize calorie burning, have your biggest meal at noon. Or if dinner is large, eat early so that your body has some time to burn these calories before going to sleep.

9. *Young women do unhealthy things to stay slim. What are the implications of this?*

A recent Statistics Canada General Social Survey reported that

36% of women who were neither too fat nor too thin said they thought they were too fat. And 25% of women in their early 20s were underweight. In contrast, only 12% of men who were in their ideal weight range believed they were overweight.

These numbers clearly reveal just how strongly women have been socialized into believing that they should look like runway models. In keeping with this belief, many of my teenage clients live almost exclusively on low-calorie foods, such as fruits and vegetables. They often avoid all protein in the belief that it is too fattening. As a result of such eating patterns, lean muscle tissue is mobilized to provide daily protein needs. (Muscle is the first storage site for protein.) Such young women are very thin, but they end up with a high percentage of body fat. Many in this group also avoid exercise, which serves only to further complicate problems of underdeveloped muscles and skin that becomes loose and flabby.

Without the addition of low-fat protein, any weight gain that occurs on such a diet will end up largely as fat. These women are malnourished but must eat a restricted diet to remain thin, so they often feel lethargic, and their reduced iron consumption — iron is found mainly in protein foods — can frequently lead to anemia. Bone loss, from the avoidance of all dairy products, can also develop. And problems for mother and fetus are common.

10. I don't want to lose 20 pounds, I want to feel 20 years younger. What can I do?

About one-third of all elderly people are in a similar situation, nutritionally speaking, to that of young women. They, too, are malnourished — although they do not sacrifice their health in a misguided effort to keep slim. Often they are underweight because they don't consume enough calories. Although some are overweight, they too are undernourished from eating predominantly empty-calorie foods. Unfortunately, either way, many elderly people are caught in a self-perpetuating situation.

As preparing complete and balanced meals becomes too much effort, poor eating patterns provide too few calories. Or the calories provide too few nutrients. This pattern saps the energy needed for regular shopping and cooking, and eventually life itself becomes a chore.

Understandably, diabetes, heart problems and a variety of commonly used medications all serve to restrict and complicate the diets of elderly people, as well as to reduce the absorption of some vitamins and minerals. Lack of teeth or poorly fitting dentures makes chewing some foods difficult. And the cost of food may be a problem. Living on one's own makes it impractical to buy many foods in bulk. Small quantities of most products are more costly, often necessitating the purchase of inexpensive brands. And more cheaply priced processed foods are usually not as healthy as upper-end choices.

There is, however, a lot of room for improvement in the diet and health status of older people. The key is to break the vicious circle of malnutrition, decreased health and more malnutrition. For example, insufficient iron consumption leads to anemia, which, compounded by loneliness and wasting muscles from inactivity, contributes to lethargy and a poor appetite. Depressed and lethargic, such people feel even less like cooking and eating properly. They're not active, so they eat less — and the circle continues.

The "tea and toast" syndrome leads to deficiencies in a variety of vitamins and minerals besides iron. It is partly for this reason that some older people are susceptible to so many colds and viruses. Headaches and dizzy spells may often be a symptom of high blood pressure, caused by years of eating fatty, high-sodium foods. Caffeinated beverages contribute to sleeping problems and mood swings, and because people's tolerance for caffeine declines with age, a little can have a large stimulating effect.

Vitamin B_{12} deficiencies not severe enough to show up in a blood test can contribute to symptoms that mimic Alzheimer's or senility. Some people will not be oriented in time or place, they don't recognize others, and they may feel tingling sensations in various parts of their bodies. Even a "low-normal" B_{12} level can cause these problems.

Our ability to process sugar decreases with age. Eating simple sugars may overwhelm the body's ability to remove sugar from the blood and lead to wide energy swings. Laxatives, such as mineral oil, when substituted for proper fibre in the diet, interfere with the absorption of fat-soluble vitamins A, D, E and K. And the spinal column sometimes degenerates from osteoporosis, causing people to shrink in stature.

All responsible researchers recommend a healthy, balanced diet as the first line of defence against the problems of ageing. And my recipes show that such a diet need not be expensive. As old age, like taxes, is preferable to the alternative, appreciate that sound nutrition can contribute toward making the latter part of our lives as enjoyable as the earlier years.

Proper nutrition will help in many ways to delay or minimize chronic constipation, fragile bones, diabetes and high blood pressure. Correct nutrition can rectify some cases of confusion, delusional thinking, memory lapses, depression and a general lack of zest for living.

Here are some suggestions:

- When your B_{12} level is low (often at the low end of the normal range), standard B_{12} injections produce benefits after a few months. Injections are more effective than tablets, as some people's digestive systems can't absorb B_{12}. It also seems that older people can't absorb B_6 as well as younger people and should eat about 20% more than the current RDA. As well, recent studies suggest that the present RDA for riboflavin is too low. Milk packaged in cardboard containers (so that light cannot penetrate) is the main source of riboflavin.
- If you do not or cannot drink much milk, ask your doctor to suggest a supplement to raise your vitamin D levels to the midpoint of the normal range.
- As we become older, cataracts or retinal damage can eventually become a significant problem. Of people 55 to 64, 5% develop cataracts. Evidence is accumulating that beta carotene and vitamins C and E delay these problems. Vitamin E also enhances immune response. It cannot be emphasized strongly enough that researchers recommend a healthy diet as the first line of defence against eye problems. Moderate supplementing also seems beneficial, but safe required doses are not yet known. At any rate, supplementation should not exceed 500 mg a day of vitamin C, 400 IU of vitamin E and 10,000 mg a day of beta carotene.

There is no end to the things that can make life seem worth living again. Once older people feel better from eating an improved diet, encourage them to see friends regularly, to get involved with community activities and to take turns making meals for one or two others. Perhaps they would enjoy teaching whatever interests them to others in retirement homes. And they should make sure that once they are active they begin to exercise. Better yet, they can start on an exercise regimen when they improve their nutrition.

Exercise — weight and aerobic training — is essential to energy and mobility. Muscles that have been underused for years and that have atrophied significantly will respond, as if by miracle, to exercise. People who have not climbed stairs for five to ten years will suddenly find that they can do so again. Seek the assistance of a professional fitness instructor for all exercise guidelines. If you live in Canada contact: 1) your local Red Cross branch; ask about their "Fun and Fitness Program"; 2) your local YM/YWCA; they usually conduct fitness classes for elderly people; 3) the recreation department or "Parks and Recreation" department of many municipal governments, which can provide a list of local fitness classes for the elderly. The sources listed here may also be able to help find instructors for those who are restricted to their homes.

11. Diet instructions always seem to include drinking 8 glasses of water per day. Is this really necessary?

High-protein diets always recommend consuming 6 to 8 glasses of water each day because water helps to flush waste products, which accumulate on such diets. This reduces the chance of developing gout, a problem for those who follow such diets. High-protein diets also are dehydrating, so they require adequate water consumption. We now know better than to attempt this fad approach to weight loss.

However, accepted medical standards suggest that during a typical day, all healthy people should drink 6 to 8 8-ounce glasses of water. But there is nothing magical in these numbers. Active people may need 12 or more glasses, and a small person with a desk job in an air-conditioned office may find that 2 suffice.

During an average day our bodies process 1.5 to 3 quarts of

water. When we are working hard in the heat, our needs increase to one quart or more per hour. We need water to keep us hydrated, to flush waste products out of our bodies, to enhance regular elimination and to regulate body temperature. We must get water from food or fluid. And food usually contributes less than one quart per day.

Among other things, being a little dehydrated reduces your energy level, so don't wait until you are thirsty to drink water. Unless you consume way too much, there is no danger, except perhaps not being able to find a convenient bathroom. Any excess water is simply passed as urine.

Water is the best source of fluid because it is absorbed easily by our tissues. Although fruit and vegetable juices rank second, fluids that are too high in sugar are not absorbed as well as water. Additionally, since such drinks don't have any fibre, blood sugar swings can be extreme. Milk is good for those who are not lactose intolerant, as it is almost 90% water. Decaffeinated soft drinks aren't bad, but for other reasons it is best to consume them in moderation. Any caffeinated beverage is dehydrating, and alcoholic beverages are so dehydrating that they're worthless.

Thirst is not always a good indication of how much water to drink. When you are really active, if it's hot or if you are at a high altitude, force yourself to drink even if you are not thirsty. Older people also should not trust their sense of thirst for an indication of how much water to drink. Ageing adversely affects our sense of thirst, and dehydration does not give much warning. Older adults report dehydration more frequently than any other group.

Water also can help minimize the food cravings people experience when losing weight. Some of us routinely misinterpret cravings for fluid as cravings for food and end up eating to satisfy thirst. Instead of gulping down a glass of water, sipping a few ounces at frequent intervals will often do the trick. Drink cool water — 40 to 50°F — not coffee or tea. While some other drinks will aid hydration, the goal is to satisfy thirst and not to stimulate your taste buds.

Finally, when you feel the symptoms of a cold or flu developing, drinking water will help to flush the virus out of your system.

12. May I eat unlimited amounts of fruit and drink fruit juices while trying to lose weight?

Many of us view fruit as a healthy snack, and people trying to lose weight frequently eat it in great quantities. Unfortunately, the sugar contained in fruit and fruit juice causes our blood sugar levels to rise. Elevated blood sugar, in turn, results in an insulin increase, and insulin slows fat metabolism. In other words, it inhibits our fat stores from being burned as fuel. For this reason, fruit should be consumed in moderation by those attempting to lose weight.

To help you compare the amount of sugar in various fruits, I have listed the amount of fruit that, on most weight-loss food exchange lists, would represent one fruit serving. The sugar content of tropical fruits, such as mango and papaya, and dried fruits is much higher than those on the list.

I prefer fresh fruit to juice. It's more filling than juice, provides important fibre and minimizes blood sugar swings that can make us feel so terrible. Apple, orange and grapefruit juices are lower in calories than other juices, such as pineapple, cranberry and grape. Sparkling waters that contain fruit juice are high in calories, often containing 125 calories per serving. If you want to drink juice on occasion, President's Choice has three flavours made with sweetener to reduce their caloric content: Pink Grapefruit, Cranberry and Cranberry/Raspberry. Also available is President's Choice Free And Clear, which is free of sugar, sodium and caffeine. Koala brand provides another juice alternative at only 60 calories per bottle.

1 SERVING FRUIT EQUIVALENTS

Apple	½ medium
Applesauce	½ cup unsweetened
Apricots	2 medium
Banana	½ small
Blueberries	½ cup
Cantaloupe	¼ medium
Cherries	½ cup
Grapefruit	½ medium
Grapes	10

Honeydew melon	1 cup
Kiwi	1 medium
Nectarine	1 medium
Orange	1 medium
Peach	1 medium
Pear	½ medium
Pineapple	½ cup (cubed)
Plum	1 large
Raspberries	½ cup
Rhubarb	1 cup cooked (without sugar)
Strawberries	¾ cup
Tangerine	1 medium
Watermelon	1 cup (cubed)

Vegetables are a better diet snack than fruit. They have a lower sugar content and therefore don't interfere with fat mobilization. Some vegetables are so low in calories (when eaten without toppings) that you can eat as much as you desire or can digest. They are just as filling as fruit or juice. The following all qualify:

alfalfa or bean sprouts	green beans
asparagus	green pepper
bamboo shoots	leeks
broccoli	lettuce
Brussels sprouts	mushrooms
cabbage	okra
cauliflower	radishes
celery	red pepper
cucumber	spinach
eggplant	zucchini

Salsa (President's Choice has 4 calories per tablespoon), President's Choice Too Good To Be True Tzatziki or Gloria vegetable spread (each at 11 calories per tablespoon) and low-cal salad dressings all make good toppings for vegetables.

13. *I see diet shakes and liquid meal replacements advertised everywhere I turn. Should I drink them?*

Oprah Winfrey lost weight on a liquid diet, but it seems that she gained it back faster than she lost it. Enough said about using these drinks as a dieting method. But what about occasionally using them to replace a meal?

Liquid meal replacements are usually fortified with vitamins and minerals, but vitamins alone won't fill you up. Furthermore, the quality of the vitamins provided in such drinks, and therefore the percentage of them you absorb, is impossible to determine. As well, most of these drinks are low in fibre, so guess what's used to fill you up? Low-quality fat. If you have one of these drinks instead of breakfast or lunch, you miss out on the insoluble fibre that a half cup of All-Bran or a healthy lunch provides.

The labels of these drinks often state that they contain fibre, but it's soluble fibre, which is not as filling as insoluble fibre. You're more apt to get hungry between meals than if you ate real food. Although instructions on some drinks recommend preparation in a blender, whipped air is not filling for very long. A few good burps and you're hungry again!

The other main ingredient in these drinks is — you guessed it — sugar. Shortly before a meal your blood sugar is at its lowest —and at its very lowest before breakfast. These mega-sugar drinks can therefore subject your blood sugar to a rapid rise and fall. By mid-morning or mid-afternoon, you've got the blood sugar blues and you're hungry, as well. That's when a doughnut and a strong coffee become particularly appealing. Why set yourself up for a temptation? Have a piece of fruit and yogurt, toast, or a whole wheat bagel — real food for real needs!

14. *I've tried to lose weight, but when I eat less I get hungry. What can I do?*

The body recognizes any significant reduction in caloric intake as a source of stress. It also can tell that there has been a change in your weight. In its wisdom it seeks to keep things stable. This tendency is known as homeostasis and keeps your metabolism from getting out of whack.

When you lose weight, the body's natural (homeostatic) reaction is to make you hungry so you will eat more and gain back the weight you lost. This hunger will pass in a few days, after you adjust to your new weight. The hunger may occur a few times during a period of weight loss, lasting up to a few days each time. Try snacking from the list of vegetables in question 13, and use a little will-power. Will-power is great for short-term problems such as this one.

15. What is the best thing for lunch when I'm in a rush?

It's not a Caesar, Greek or julienne salad. But if you eat at work keep a bottle of low-cal dressing in the fridge for those garden salads you should eat. Hot dogs are a bad choice, as well. (See the answer to question 16.) But carnivores will be happy to know that a sliced chicken or turkey (without the skin) or low-fat ham sandwich on whole grain bread is the best choice. Hold the butter, hold the mayo. Use lettuce, tomato, cucumber, sprouts and mustard for flavour.

Several delicatessens now have Heart Smart programs, which include a choice of sandwiches — low-fat meats, and tuna, salmon and egg made with light mayo. They may also use coho salmon, which is lower in fat than sockeye salmon. Choose light or dark rye or other grainy breads.

16. Are "all beef" hot dogs okay?

Here is a great example of creative advertising. The beef in these hot dogs and in a "100% beef" hot dog is "all beef." Just as the veal or turkey in an "all veal" hot dog or "all turkey" hot dog is "100%" all veal or all turkey. However, the meat portion seldom accounts for more than 25 to 30% — in some cases only 10% — of the total content of the hot dog. The other 70 to 75% is mainly fat from skin and sometimes other questionable parts of the animal. You can be sure that we're not talking sirloin or free range here. The cuts are usually bargain basement specials. Thinking about these ingredients when you get a craving for a hot dog will help to curb it!

In a typical 2-ounce "all beef" hot dog, there are 184 calories; up to 150 of these derive from fat. If you want to eat a hot dog, try the new lower-fat alternatives. But beware, these products still

PHOTO: Roasted Eggplant and Pepper Salad (page 174); Wild Rice and Turkey Salad (page 173)

contain considerable amounts of fat (and sodium), so eat them only occasionally. For those of you who are more adventurous, there are several brands of tofu hot dogs on the market. These contain polyunsaturated fat instead of the saturated fat found in the alternatives. I particularly like the President's Choice Too Good To Be True "No Meat" veggie dogs. Once you add mustard, ketchup, onions or other low-cal toppings they really taste as good as "all beef" choices.

17. *Which is better for me, butter or margarine?*

Margarine was supposed to be a breakthrough in the nutritional campaign against heart disease. So, what went wrong? Vegetable oils are liquid at room temperature, and margarine is made from vegetable oil. Most margarine manufacturers hydrogenate the oil to give it a creamy texture. The harder the margarine comes out, the greater the degree of hydrogenation. For this reason tub margarines are preferable to stick margarines.

The problem is that the process of hydrogenation transforms the oil into a more saturated fat. Studies have found that these fats raise total cholesterol and reduce the HDL, or good, cholesterol. Additionally, some preliminary investigations suggest that they may compromise our immune systems.

Butter and margarine have the same number of calories. Butter, although a saturated fat, is a natural product and usually has not had chemical colouring added to it. It does not seem, to my way of thinking, that one choice is better. No matter what choice you make, use a minimal amount. Most people like the taste of butter over margarine, and therefore probably will find themselves satisfied using a smaller quantity of butter rather than margarine to impart flavour.

The three foods that most frequently call for butter or margarine are bread or toast, baked potatoes and vegetables. Grainier breads are usually better-tasting than refined white breads and are great without any topping. By using a bit of President's Choice Twice the Fruit jam on toast, or making sandwiches more tasty with condiments, you won't miss the fat. Baked potatoes are delicious with toppings such as Dijon mustard, low-fat tzatziki (recipe on page 150), salsa, cottage cheese, yogurt and dill, and Molly

PHOTO: *Grilled Vegetable Lasagna (page 196)*

McButter (although it won't melt on toast).

When cooking, I replace both butter and margarine with environmentally friendly cooking spray whenever I can. You will see examples of this substitution in my recipes. I sauté things such as onions on the stove or in the microwave in a little water, instead of fat. In some situations, wine or a little chicken or vegetable stock imparts a better taste when sautéing.

If your diet is generally low in fat and you want to use butter or margarine, go ahead, but moderation is the key. You may want to try the whipped butters or margarines, as they have half the calories and fat of the regular varieties. Just make sure you don't use twice as much! Whatever you do, don't fry with margarine. The heat changes the fatty acids into a form that is damaging to your blood vessels. If you must fry with fat, use a healthy vegetable oil. (See the chart on page 26.)

18. How can I suppress my cravings for sweets?

Some food cravings can be addictions and are hard to extinguish. It takes commitment and will-power. To succeed, you must go on the wagon for an extended period. Twelve weeks seems to be the minimum time required to adjust successfully to new habits. Less intense cravings can be triggered by physical or emotional factors such as fatigue, stress and depression. It is difficult not to get a craving when you walk past a bakery — even when you're not hungry. If you become aware of the foods you crave and the situations that get you into trouble, you will find it easier to work out a strategy of avoidance.

When I tell my clients to go on the wagon, I always look for alternatives. When you get a craving for something sweet and you are truly hungry, don't deny yourself completely. It is better to have an appropriate alternative.

- An apple does not substitute for a Danish, but a piece of whole wheat toast with cinnamon and Splenda brand sweetener, or some Twice The Fruit jam, will.
- Cut-up vegetables don't satisfy a craving for chocolate cake, but light hot chocolate or diet Fudgsicles often do the trick.
- Don't buy bags of cookies, but instead buy one or two from a

health food store — after you read the label.

- Don't eat dessert immediately after a meal. People usually do so out of habit, not hunger. Give yourself one hour to digest. Then, if you're still hungry, have a snack.
- If you're not hungry but have a craving for sweets, chew sugarless gum, or try a diet pop or a glass of water. I find that the best trick is to brush my teeth. When my mouth feels fresh, I don't need anything to mask the flavour of the last food I ate.

Eating a balanced diet also will help to reduce cravings. Psychological cravings occur when we are not hungry, and we can often satisfy them with relaxation, meditation, sex or physical activities. These diversions and delays won't work for all of us all of the time, but they can help us to reduce the amount of junk food we regularly consume. They also can be a lot more fun.

19. I often snack on popcorn at night, as I understand that it is low in calories. Is this true?

Popcorn is generally touted over potato chips and other similar snack foods because it's popped and not fried. But most people, thinking it's low-cal, eat a large bowl instead of eating a smaller portion of another snack food. Some people even eat it as an alternative to dinner.

Popcorn is corn, a carbohydrate. It offers little nutritional value, so it doesn't replace nutrient-rich carbohydrate servings such as grains or pasta. And this empty-calorie food is not necessarily low-cal. The unbuttered popcorn typically served at movie houses is cooked in fat and has about 50 calories per cup. Most people think that a small bag is one or two cups. It's usually nine, and hides 450 calories — without topping! A medium box is 12 cups and a large is 16 cups. Amazing how small indulgences add up.

If you make your own popcorn, try air popped (about 35 calories per popped cup) or a brand like Orville Redenbacher's Light, which is also low in sodium. A great alternative is rice crackers, at only 7 calories per cracker. Or try Guiltless Gourmet tortilla chips, which are baked instead of fried. They have 8 calories per chip. Remember, if you're hungry, 2 cups of popcorn or 10 chips will not do the trick. Eat these foods as a snack and not as a meal.

If I don't have time for dinner before a movie, I take a sandwich and some cut-up vegetables to the show.

20. What can I do about heartburn?

Heartburn, or acid indigestion, results when stomach acids back up into the esophagus. There are several causes of this burning pain. Some are congenital. But eating fatty and spicy foods, drinking too much coffee or alcohol (particularly on an empty stomach), smoking cigarettes, wearing pants or a skirt that are too tight and being overweight all contribute. If you frequently experience acid indigestion, don't eat when you are aggravated and don't lie down to rest after meals. If you get heartburn at night, elevate the head of your bed about 6 inches, and try to finish dinner about three hours before going to sleep.

Clients of mine who are overweight find that weight loss relieves the pressure that causes a portion of the stomach to force its way up through the diaphragm (a hiatus hernia). Losing weight also allows them to cease medication for the condition. One in 10 North Americans gets heartburn, and one in eight takes antacids at least once a week. I am frequently told that weight loss enables people to stop taking antacids. Continued self-medication for this problem is not without risk of side effects.

Finally, mistaking chest pain for heartburn can be a serious error. If you get heartburn more than very occasionally, consult your doctor (or perhaps a specialist who is trained to determine whether your symptoms are heartburn or something more serious).

21. Why do I often get headaches when I'm dieting?

There are three likely reasons. When we diet, some of us try to cut back on caffeinated beverages. Caffeine is a drug, and withdrawal can cause headaches that may last for seven to 10 days. Cut back gradually, tough it out and don't overdo the Tylenol. (The new gel caps work very quickly for some people.)

Reduced food consumption leads to less sodium intake, as most foods contain at least some sodium. When you reduce the amount that you eat and begin to eat fewer processed foods, the decreased salt intake leads to less fluid retention, which lowers your blood volume and therefore reduces your blood pressure. On occasion reduced blood pressure may cause headaches, dizziness or weakness. These symptoms lead some people to think that they need sugar, when they actually require sodium. Try eating a quarter teaspoon of salt (either on your food or in a glass of water).

When dieting, people often drink more water than they would otherwise. The resulting increase in urination can cause potassium, a water-soluble mineral, to be flushed out of the system. An abnormally low potassium level can cause the above symptoms. So if the symptoms don't disappear within 20 minutes of ingesting salt, have an orange or a banana, fruits that provide substantial amounts of potassium.

22. What can I do to feel better around the time of my menstrual cycle?

During this time many women crave sweets, become constipated or feel tired and irritable. I recommend dietary changes to my clients. These changes make a world of difference to the vast majority of them.

It's a common lament: "The week before my period I'm absolutely driven to eat sweets and junk food, yet at other times I have a lot of self-control." This problem is not your fault — at least 20% of women turn to sweets and junk food at this time in their cycle. You can blame your hormones. Between ovulation and menstruation the hormone progesterone increases, causing a reduction in blood sugar, which may lead to cravings. The sugary snack, in turn, causes your blood sugar to rise rapidly. Insulin then clears it from your blood, and the return to low blood sugar causes another craving.

Eating a well-balanced diet all month long helps to prevent premenstrual bingeing. As well, consider the times of day that you usually binge and plan distractions that make you physically active. Getting out of the house and away from the kitchen can help. Some people will find that raw fruits and vegetables are fairly good alternatives to sugary snack foods at these times. Fruit contains sugar, but the fibre in it slows absorption into the blood, preventing the insulin-led blood sugar crash. If you really need something sweet, eat a Fudgsicle Light, a Creamsicle Light or whole grain toast with "all fruit" jam.

Some women have worse cravings than others because their bodies produce more progesterone. If you are subject to particularly bad cravings, try to keep your blood sugar levels more constant.

This is easily achieved by eating smaller meals more frequently. Try six small meals a day and minimize or eliminate your caffeine consumption. Caffeine also contributes to excessive blood sugar swings.

Constipation is a common occurrence during the premenstrual period. To minimize symptoms, eat adequate amounts of complex carbohydrates and drink plenty of water. Make sure that your fibre intake is sufficient, as well. Just ½ cup of All-Bran provides 10 grams of fibre. After one or two cycles of better eating, the vast majority of my clients loosen up substantially.

Those of you who experience uncomfortable bloating and premenstrual depression should benefit from taking up to 50 mg of vitamin B$_6$ and a multi-B vitamin each day. Be sure that total B$_6$ intake does not exceed 50 mg. I like the natural brands of these vitamins, such as Jamieson or Swiss Herbal, as they seem to be absorbed through the intestinal wall most completely. Also, be sure to consume adequate amounts (60 mg to 100 mg) of vitamin C.

Premenstrual bloating and weight gain, cramps and headaches are often related to sodium retention. Try a low-sodium diet for a week to 10 days before your period is due. If you seem to be unusually tired, you may have a very heavy blood flow that depletes you of iron. Menstruating women aged 18 to 50 have the highest need for iron but often do not consume enough in their diets. If you bleed heavily, raise your iron intake by eating low-fat animal protein during menstruation. The "heme" form of iron in this type of protein is absorbed more efficiently than the iron in plant sources. By eating a food that is high in vitamin C, such as a baked potato, tomato or green pepper along with the high-iron food, the absorption of iron increases.

Finally, some women experience these symptoms in mid-cycle, in other words when they are ovulating. At this time an elevated estrogen level can be responsible for discomfort. Women following my guidelines all month long will find mid-cycle symptoms minimized.

23. *What is cellulite, and how can I get rid of it?*

The unsightly dimples and ripples that appear on the thighs and buttocks of women have been labelled "cellulite." We are told it's a special kind of fat that's hard to get rid of and requires special treatment. But the only thing that creams, injections and visits to cellulite salons will do is make your wallet lighter.

Cellulite is merely good old fat. Much body fat is stored direct-ly beneath the skin, where strands of connective fibre separate fat cells into compartments. Women are more susceptible than men to the look known as cellulite, because they carry more fat in these areas and often have thinner skin. Men also have a thicker network of fibrous connective tissue in the skin, which helps it maintain a more uniform tone.

However, having this fat propensity does not forever doom your bum and thighs. When the fat cells increase in size from weight gain, they bulge out of the compartments, giving the appearance of cellulite. Lack of physical fitness also results in less body tone, allowing the fat to bulge more easily.

You can't spot-reduce fat, no matter where it is — and we all carry it in different places. Getting rid of the cellulite look involves the same process as reducing fat anywhere else on the body. Eat a low-fat diet, participate in regular aerobic exercise and do some weight or resistance training. Aerobic exercise and a healthy diet minimize body fat, allowing the underlying muscle to show through. Weight training tones and firms muscles, making exposed muscle look better. Give it a few months, and most of you will see a change. If there are still no results and the issue is important to you, even though the rest of your body now looks great, your only alternative is to consult a plastic surgeon.

24. Well, cellulite treatments don't work. But can electric muscle stimulators make me thin?

Many studies have shown that these machines produce no sig-nificant change in body weight or fat. Your body doesn't selec-tively draw energy from fat stores in the parts being exercised or electrically stimulated. As you exercise, your body draws on fat from all areas. You cannot spot-reduce or eliminate fat from a cer-tain part of your body by exercising that part alone. The electric muscle stimulator was designed to prevent muscle atrophy in injured athletes during their recovery period. After they recover, athletes begin to exercise again; they don't use the machine as a substitute for exercise.

Part IV
NOTES TO RECIPES

To get you started on your new nutritional lifestyle, this part of the book contains 143 recipes that will make healthy eating enjoyable. While we should endeavour to consume 55% of our daily calories in the form of carbohydrate, 15% as protein and no more than 30% from fat, it is acceptable to eat individual items that are more than 30% fat. And some of my recipes contain more than 30% of their calories as fat.

The goal is to plan your daily fat consumption, not to be obsessive about everything you eat. If, for example, you have a low-fat breakfast and lunch, a slightly higher fat dinner is okay. Or, if your main course has 50% calories from fat, as is common in meat dishes, include vegetables and a salad with the meal. Provided that by the end of the day calories from protein, carbohydrate and fat are balanced in the above ratios, you are eating sensibly.

Also take note that some of my sauces and dressings are above 30% fat content, but so much lower in calories than the regular alternatives that you end up consuming less than one-half the fat and calories you would otherwise. And the number of calories you consume from such sources will still be a very small percentage of total daily caloric intake.

Similarly, the desserts in this book contain above 30% calories from fat. But again, they have only half (or fewer) calories and fat than the conventional recipe, and none of the sugar. There is no reason why an occasional dessert, consumed in moderation, can't be part of a healthy eating plan.

For further simplification, with a few exceptions, I have coded each recipe into at least one of the following categories: Very Easy to Prepare, Gourmet, Microwavable, Economical and Freezable. All recipes are my own, a result of my love for cooking and several years of experimenting with alternatives to fat, salt, sugar and highly processed ingredients.

RECIPE SYMBOLS

North Americans frequently take the attitude that if something is not immoral, hazardous or fattening, then it's not fun. I hope my recipes change this mindset. I have included a symbol below the title of each recipe. The legend is as follows:

Very Easy to Prepare: These recipes take only a few minutes to prepare, and ingredients are available almost anywhere.

⚒

Gourmet: Great for company, since the dishes are especially attractive to look at as well as more complex or distinct in taste.

≋

Microwavable: This means a dish is microwaved from beginning to end, not that one stage is prepared in the microwave or that the dish can be heated in the microwave.

💲

Economical: These dishes can be prepared at a low cost and include ingredients you are likely to have on hand.

❄

Freezable: These dishes can be frozen, either in individual servings or in family-size portions.

The best way to freeze food is to wrap it in individual airtight portions and place them near the edge of the freezer. When they are frozen, double wrap them. If time or freezer space does not permit this, cool the food and double wrap it in airtight wrapping. Plastic containers are great for freezing individual servings of soup.

COOKING SUGGESTIONS

- I use fresh garlic and ginger in my cooking, as it tastes best. However, I feel that President's Choice (PC) Chopped Garlic in Oil and PC Puréed Ginger are great time-saving alternatives. Equivalent measures are:

½ teaspoon garlic in oil = 1 fresh clove

1 teaspoon pureed ginger = 1 teaspoon fresh

- When you use bouillon or chicken broths and stocks, it is always best to use homemade stock that has been refrigerated and then had the fat removed. If you do not have stock on hand, the powdered bouillon available in bulk at health food stores (it is yellow with parsley flecks in it and does not contain MSG) or President's Choice fresh chicken or beef stock concentrates are good alternatives. However, if you are on a low-salt diet, a homemade stock would be preferable, as commercially made products are high in sodium.
- A stovetop grill, such as that made by President's Choice, is great for cooking things like eggplant, zucchini and turkey burgers.
- Some recipes call for pressed tofu. This is a denser tofu that will not fall apart when stir-fried.
- In many recipes, I use cooking spray instead of oil. A light misting is all that is necessary to stop items from sticking. Saturating the surface serves only to add fat calories to the dish.
- Wherever soy sauce is called for in recipes, you may want to use low-sodium soy sauce. It has half the sodium of regular varieties. Several brands are available.
- I don't peel skins from vegetables unless, of course, they've been waxed. The skins contain lots of vitamins and fibre. To remove pesticides and insecticides, use a fruit and vegetable safety rinse such as Dr. Browner's (which can be found in health food stores, pharmacies or supermarkets).

WHAT'S SO GREAT ABOUT SPLENDA?

Splenda brand sweetener was developed in 1976 and is the first low-calorie sweetener created from sugar. And it tastes like sugar, with no unpleasant aftertaste. The product is known generically as sucralose. The manufacturing process modifies sugar to produce a calorie-free substance that is 600 times as sweet as sugar.

Over the past 15 years Splenda has passed 100 studies to show that it is safe to eat and 40 studies to show that it is safe for the environment. The World Health Organization has pronounced it safe, and pregnant women can safely consume it.

It is substituted one-for-one where sugar is called for, but has only 2 calories per teaspoon as opposed to 16 to 18 calories in a teaspoon of sugar. Overall it is more desirable for low-cal cooking than any other sweetening agent currently available and it is compatible with all food ingredients. Unlike synthetic sweeteners, it does not break down when heated in cooking. It has a very long shelf life. It is also a particularly good substitute for those who get headaches from Aspartame.

Too Good To Be True Sweet and Sour Sauce was the first Canadian product to be made with Splenda. Splenda will soon be available in many products, so consumers will be able to reduce their sugar and total caloric consumption.

Cooking with Splenda

- Store Splenda in a cool, dry place away from moisture and heat.
- Some Splenda baked goods do not become deep golden brown, so do not consider browning as a signal for doneness. Instead, test by inserting a wooden pick in the centre; if it comes out clean, the food is done. Check for doneness 5 to 10 minutes sooner than baking time for recipes using sugar.
- For cakes, sugar not only sweetens but gives structure and volume. Cakes are a delicate balance of ingredients, so some experimentation may be necessary on your own recipes. The mixing and baking procedure for your cake recipe should be modified as follows:
  - Beat the fat with an electric beater on high speed for 1 minute.
  - Add eggs and flavouring and beat for 30 seconds.
  - Sift together all dry ingredients, including Splenda. Add alternately with liquid in three additions, mixing on low for 30 seconds to 1 minute with each addition.
  - Check for doneness 5 to 10 minutes sooner than the recipe calls for.
- The sugar content of fudge, caramel and other candy, angel food and pound cake, and meringues is generally much too high and provides an important structural component that does not allow substitution with Splenda. The use of Splenda in these recipes is not recommended.

• If you have questions or comments, call the Splenda hot line at 1-800-561-0070.

TOO GOOD TO BE TRUE EATING

President's Choice Too Good To Be True products are superior in many ways to competing brands. For example, they are low in fat and preservatives, and several are high in fibre. Either very little sugar is used or Splenda brand sweetener replaces sugar. Some items will spice up your meals, and others are complete meals in themselves. New products are constantly being added to the line; some unique and outstanding examples follow:

Dehydrated soups: Spicy Black Bean, Split Pea, Lentil With Curry, Chili, Leek and Potato, Minestrone, Cajun Beans and Rice

Frozen vegetarian meals: Lasagna, Chili, Mushroom Cheese Rounds, "No Meat" veggie dogs

No Oil Added salad dressings: Mustard Tarragon, Raspberry, Curry, Mango

Sauces: Gourmet Barbecue Sauce, Spicy Thai, Szechwan Peanut, Sweet and Sour, Hong Kong Black Bean and Garlic, Salsa Pasta Sauce, Tzatziki Yogurt Dip and Spread, Memories of Singapore, Memories of Canton

Baked goods: Multigrain, Bran loaf and 11 Reasons (bread), Muesli Muffins

Cereals: Ancient Grains and 7 Reasons

Dessert: Tofu Almond Dessert

Miscellaneous: Lemon Herb Seasoning, Beta Blast Betacarotene Cocktail

Cinnamon and Vanilla Glazed French Toast

⏱ 💲

The addition of cinnamon and vanilla to this dish gives it a rich and buttery taste, without adding any fat. Serve the toast with a spoonful of all-fruit jam or President's Choice Twice The Fruit jam.

- 1 egg white
- 1 egg
- ½ cup skim milk
- 1 teaspoon vanilla
- 1 teaspoon cinnamon
- 1 teaspoon nutmeg
- 4 slices bread

1. Combine all ingredients except bread in flat bowl or pie plate. Beat well.

2. Soak each slice of bread in mixture, turning to coat both sides.

3. Spray non-stick pan with cooking spray and place over medium-high heat. Fry each slice of soaked bread on both sides until glaze has set and toast is lightly browned.

Makes 2 servings. PER SERVING: *Calories: 188, Protein: 12.2 g, Carbohydrates: 27.2 g, Fat: 4.1 g, % Cal. from fat: 19*

Salsa Omelette

💲

Substituting egg whites for a second egg halves the cholesterol and fat content of this omelette. Use President's Choice Salsa if it is available; it is delicious and contains only 4 calories per tablespoon. Many other salsas without added oil and sugar are also available.

1 egg
2 egg whites
¼ cup mild salsa

1. Beat together egg and egg whites.

2. Spray a small skillet with cooking spray, and place over medium heat. Pour in egg mixture, and cook until eggs are partially set.

3. Spoon salsa on one side of omelette, fold omelette in half, and cook until set.

Makes 1 serving. PER SERVING: *Calories: 124, Protein: 14 g, Carbohydrates: 4.4 g, Fat: 5.1 g, % Cal. from fat: 38*

Egg and Cheese Soufflé

⚒ 💲

Make this special breakfast on a weekend or when you have a bit of extra time. A soft bread works better in this recipe than a grainy or rye loaf

2 ounces low-fat cheese
2 slices bread, quartered
2 eggs
1 cup skim milk
½ teaspoon ground nutmeg
¼ teaspoon paprika
Pinch salt and pepper

1. Place cheese and bread in food processor with steel blade. Process for 5 seconds.

2. Add remaining ingredients and process with 3 on/off bursts.

3. Divide mixture evenly between two individual-size soufflé dishes sprayed with cooking spray.

4. Bake at 375°F for 25 to 30 minutes, or until golden and puffy. Serve immediately.

Makes 2 servings. PER SERVING: *Calories: 235, Protein: 19.6 g, Carbohydrates: 19.6 g, Fat: 7.6 g, % Cal. from fat:31*

Breakfast Cheese Pudding

🕐 $ ❄

This pudding makes a great breakfast when served with fresh fruit. Or enjoy it as an afternoon snack or a dessert.

    8 ounces tofu
    2 eggs
    ⅔ cup low-fat (1%) cottage cheese
    ¼ cup Splenda sweetener
    1 teaspoon vanilla
    1 teaspoon cinnamon

1. Combine all ingredients in a food processor or blender. Process until smooth.

2. Pour mixture into a loaf pan sprayed with cooking spray.

3. Bake at 350°F for 35 to 40 minutes, or until set.

4. Cool, then refrigerate. Serve cold.

Makes 4 servings. PER SERVING: *Calories: 148, Protein: 17 g, Carbohydrates: 3.8 g, Fat: 7.8 g, % Cal. from fat: 46*

Kashi Pudding

❄

Both ready-to-eat Puffed Kashi and Kashi Pilaf cereals are available at most health food stores. This recipe uses Kashi Pilaf, which must be cooked before it is added to the other ingredients.

    1 cup cooked Kashi Pilaf cereal
    1 egg
    1 cup low-fat (1%) cottage cheese
    ¾ cup plain low-fat yogurt
    ¼ cup Splenda sweetener
    ¼ cup raisins
    1 teaspoon vanilla
    1 teaspoon cinnamon

1. Combine all ingredients and mix well. Pour into a 9-inch square baking pan sprayed with cooking spray.

2. Bake at 350°F for 45 minutes.

Makes 6 servings. PER SERVING: *Calories: 138, Protein: 7.7 g, Carbohydrates: 21.2 g, Fat: 2.1 g, % Cal. from fat: 14*

Kashi and Apple Casserole

This great breakfast can be served warm or cold with a dollop of plain low-fat yogurt or a scoop of cottage cheese.

2   cups cooked Kashi Pilaf cereal
1   medium apple, unpeeled, cored and diced
⅓ cup apple juice
2   tablespoons Splenda sweetener
2   teaspoons lemon juice
1   teaspoon vanilla
½ teaspoon cinnamon

1. Combine all ingredients and mix well. Put in a 2-quart casserole sprayed with cooking spray.

2. Loosely cover with foil, and bake at 375°F for 45 minutes.

Makes 6 servings. PER SERVING: *Calories: 138, Protein: 0.31 g, Carbohydrates: 30.2 g, Fat: 0.88 g, % Cal. from fat: 6*

Skim Milk Ricotta Cheesecake

❄

Here is a breakfast for those accustomed to something sweet in the morning, for example a Danish. It also makes a great dessert. Serve with fresh berries sprinkled on top.

⅔ cup graham wafer crumbs
1 ½ tablespoons Splenda sweetener
2 tablespoons melted margarine or butter
1 pound part-skim ricotta cheese
⅓ cup plain low-fat yogurt
¼ cup Splenda sweetener
2 eggs
1 teaspoon cinnamon
1 teaspoon vanilla

1. Combine graham wafer crumbs with sweetener and margarine. Mix well.

2. Press crumb mixture evenly over the bottom of a 9-inch pie plate. Bake at 350°F for 5 minutes. Let cool.

3. Reduce oven temperature setting to 300°F. Combine remaining ingredients in food processor or blender and blend until smooth.

4. Pour mixture over crumb crust. Bake at 300°F for 40 minutes.

5. Cool, then refrigerate.

Makes 8 servings. PER SERVING: *Calories: 151, Protein: 9.0 g, Carbohydrates: 8.3 g, Fat: 9.1 g, % Cal. from fat: 54*

Apple Flan

❄ $

Make this dish ahead and freeze it. Then, on a cold morning, simply microwave it and serve it warm with a scoop of low-fat cottage cheese or yogurt on top.

3 large Matsu or spy apples, peeled, cored and sliced
2 tablespoons lemon juice
1 teaspoon cinnamon
1½ cups skim milk
2 egg whites
1 egg
¼ cup Splenda sweetener
1 teaspoon vanilla

1. Place sliced apples in large bowl and toss with lemon juice and cinnamon.

2. In another bowl, combine remaining ingredients.

3. Place apple mixture in pie plate sprayed with cooking spray. Pour milk mixture over.

4. Bake at 350°F for 50 minutes, or until custard is set. Let sit 10 to 15 minutes before serving.

Makes 6 servings. PER SERVING: *Calories: 77, Protein: 4.4 g, Carbohydrates: 13.1 g, Fat: 1.1 g, % Cal. from fat: 13*

Blender Breakfast

When berries are at their peak, serve this terrific summer breakfast in a glass or a bowl. It is delicious with a whole wheat bagel.

1½ cups plain low-fat yogurt
8 fresh strawberries*
½ cup fresh blueberries*
1 teaspoon vanilla

1. Put all ingredients in blender or food processor. Process until smooth.

* Frozen unsweetened berries can be used

Makes 2 servings. PER SERVING: *Calories: 158, Protein: 10.5 g, Carbohydrates: 22.8 g, Fat: 3.2 g, % Cal. from fat: 18*

Honey Mustard Dip

⏱ $

A delicious dip for times when friends drop by unexpectedly and you have raw vegetables but no dip. You can easily double or triple the recipe for a large crowd.

½ cup low-fat yogurt
½ cup honey mustard

1. Combine yogurt and mustard and blend well.

Makes 1 cup. PER 2 TABLESPOON SERVING: *Calories: 26, Protein: 1.0 g, Carbohydrates: 4.4 g, Fat: 0.5 g, % Cal. from fat: 17*

Tuna and Bean Dip

This dip also makes a good sandwich filling. Add some lettuce and toma-to and serve on a whole wheat pita.

1 6.5-ounce can water-packed tuna, rinsed and drained
1 cup white kidney beans (cannellini), rinsed and drained
1 small stalk celery, chopped
⅓ cup chopped red onion
1 tablespoon lemon juice
1 tablespoon prepared mustard
1 teaspoon olive oil
Pepper to taste

1. Combine tuna and beans and mash with a fork.

2. Add remaining ingredients and mix well.

Makes approximately 2 cups. PER ¼ CUP SERVING: *Calories: 73, Protein: 8.3 g, Carbohydrates: 6.7 g, Fat: 1.3 g, % Cal. from fat: 17*

Eggplant Dip

Many eggplant dishes are high in calories because eggplant absorbs a lot of oil. This dip does not contain any oil. It's great as an appetizer with raw vegetables and whole grain crackers, or as a condiment with meat, fish or poultry.

1 large eggplant (approximately 2 pounds)
2 medium onions, sliced
3 to 4 cloves garlic, minced
1 19-ounce can tomatoes
¼ cup tomato sauce
3 tablespoons balsamic vinegar
1 tablespoon oregano
1 teaspoon basil
1 bay leaf

1. Cut eggplant in half lengthwise. Bake at 400°F for 30 to 40 minutes, or until soft. Let cool.

2. Scoop out the flesh of eggplant and dice.

3. Place onions in bowl with 3 tablespoons water. Cook, covered, in microwave on High for 3 minutes.

4. Add onions and any remaining water in bowl to minced garlic in a large non-stick skillet. Sauté 1 minute.

5. Add remaining ingredients to skillet. Cover and simmer for 30 minutes. Let cool. Remove bay leaf.

6. Purée in food processor or blender until chunky.

Makes 6 cups. PER ¼ CUP SERVING: *Calories: 10, Protein: 0.43 g, Carbohydrates: 2.2 g, Fat: 0.07 g, % Cal. from fat: 6*

Tzatziki Cucumber Dip

🕐 ✕ $

My favourite dip for raw vegetables is Too Good To Be True (TGTBT) Tzatziki dip. Here's a recipe that comes pretty close. TGTBT Tzatziki has 11 calories per tablespoon, this recipe has 15, but the regular variety has up to 40 calories per tablespoon.

½ English cucumber, peeled, seeded and chopped
2   cloves garlic, minced
3   tablespoons chopped fresh dill
¾   cup plain low-fat yogurt
½   cup light mayonnaise
Salt and pepper to taste

1. Combine all ingredients in a bowl.

2. Cover and refrigerate at least 1 hour to ensure that flavours blend.

Makes 2 cups. PER 2 TABLESPOON SERVING: *Calories: 30, Protein: 0.65 g, Carbohydrates: 2.4 g, Fat: 2.1 g, % Cal. from fat: 60*

Bean Dip

🕐 $

Traditional bean dip recipes use sour cream to make them creamy. To lower the fat in this recipe, I've replaced the sour cream with tofu. If you don't have time to soak the black beans, this dip can also be made with TGTBT Precooked 7 Bean Mix.

1½ cups cooked black beans*
3   tablespoons lemon juice
1   tablespoon olive oil
2   teaspoons ground cumin
1   teaspoon salt
8   ounces tofu

1. Combine all ingredients in food processor. Puree until smooth.

*Just ¾ cup dry black beans soaked overnight and cooked in 3 cups water will yield 1½ cups cooked beans. Cooking time will be approximately 1 hour and 15 minutes.

Makes approximately 2 cups. PER ¼ CUP SERVING: *Calories: 40, Protein: 2.5 g, Carbohydrates: 4.3 g, Fat: 1.62 g, % Cal. from fat: 34*

Steamed Artichoke with Tzatziki Dip

A medium-sized artichoke has only 70 calories and makes a great appetizer or side dish. Dip the leaves into TGTBT Tzatziki or my Tzatziki Dip instead of the traditional lemon butter and save a lot of calories. Another advantage to artichokes is the length of time it takes to eat them. Everyone slows down to enjoy the meal!

4 medium-size artichokes, trimmed
1 cup Tzatziki Dip (page 150)

1. Place metal steamer or steaming rack in a large pot. Add a few inches of water.

2. Place artichokes on steamer. Cover pot and bring water to a boil. Cook for 25 minutes, or until artichokes are tender and leaves pull out easily. Check to ensure water does not boil away; add more if needed.

3. Serve each artichoke with ¼ cup tzatziki.

Makes 4 servings. PER SERVING: *Calories: 191, Protein: 6.9 g, Carbohydrates: 21.7 g, Fat: 10.2 g, % Cal. from fat: 45*

Roasted Garlic

⊙ ✖ $

This simple recipe makes an inexpensive gourmet appetizer that is low in calories. Once cooked, the garlic will turn very soft and the flesh can be easily removed from the skin with a sharp paring knife. If you prefer to eat the garlic "straight up," just use your teeth. I love roasted garlic spread on raw or steamed vegetables and on crackers. It also makes a nice garnish for Asparagus Salad (page 175).

4 large whole heads garlic

1. Cut four squares of aluminum foil (double-strength foil is best) and place one whole head of garlic on each piece. Sprinkle with water. Bring edges of foil together and fold to make a tightly sealed package.

2. Bake at 375°F for 1 hour.

Makes 4 servings. PER SERVING: *Calories: 44, Protein: 1.9 g, Carbohydrates: 9.9 g, Fat: 0.15 g, % Cal. from fat: 3*

Eggplant and Goat Cheese Rounds

⊙ ✖

I often split this recipe with my husband for dinner. Served with a salad and a whole grain bread, it makes a nice light meal. Most cheese shops carry low-fat goat cheese as an alternative to the rich French varieties — which are 50% fat.

1 eggplant (about 1 ½ pounds), unpeeled, sliced into ¼-inch rounds
¼ cup tomato sauce
6 ounces low-fat goat cheese
1 tablespoon oregano

1. Place sliced eggplant on a cookie sheet sprayed with cooking spray.

2. Spread small amount of tomato sauce on each slice. Crumble goat cheese on top of sauce. Sprinkle with oregano.

3. Bake at 350°F for 15 minutes and then put under broiler for 5 minutes, or until cheese is melted and bubbly.

Makes 4 appetizers or 2 main-course servings. PER APPETIZER SERVING: *Calories: 136, Protein: 6.7 g, Carbohydrates: 12.2 g, Fat: 7.6, % Cal. from fat: 47*

Hummus

☑ $

Hummus typically contains a large amount of fat and can have up to 100 calories per tablespoon. This recipe replaces some of the oil with water and lemon juice.

1½ cups drained canned chick peas
¼ cup water
1 clove garlic, minced
3 tablespoons lemon juice
1 tablespoon tahini*
1 teaspoon olive oil
½ teaspoon ground cumin

1. Combine all ingredients in food processor or blender. Purée until smooth.

*Tahini is made from ground sesame seeds and is commonly found in health food stores.

Makes approximately 1½ cups. PER 2 TABLESPOON SERVING: *Calories: 45, Protein: 2.0 g, Carbohydrates: 6.2 g, Fat: 1.5 g, % Cal. from fat: 30*

Carrot Ginger Soup

✖ $ ❄

I serve guests a 1-cup portion of this light soup. Because it is puréed, its consistency is like that of a thick cream soup.

- 4 cups chicken broth
- 6 large carrots, sliced
- 1 large onion, sliced
- 2 cloves garlic, minced
- 2 tablespoons finely minced ginger

Dash pepper

1. Combine in soup pot broth, carrots, onion, garlic and ginger. Cover and bring to a boil, then simmer partially covered for 15 minutes, stirring occasionally.

2. Process in food processor until smooth. Add pepper.

Makes 6 cups. PER 1 CUP SERVING: *Calories: 74, Protein: 4.6 g, Carbohydrates: 11.5 g, Fat: 1.1 g, % Cal. from fat: 14*

"Miracle" Soup

🕐 $ ❄

My clients call this soup a miracle because it is simple to make, tasty and very filling. At 3 or 4 o'clock, when they're feeling hungry, they heat a cup of it in the microwave, and it holds them over until dinner time.

- 1 48-ounce can tomato juice
- 2 cups beef broth
- 1 2.2 pound package frozen "California Style" vegetables*

1. Combine all ingredients in soup pot. Simmer 20 minutes.

*Although I usually prefer fresh vegetables, the frozen variety taste fine in this soup and they keep preparation time to a minimum.

Makes 12 cups. PER 1 CUP SERVING: *Calories: 45, Protein: 2.9 g, Carbohydrates: 9.7 g, Fat: 0.28 g, % Cal. from fat: 5*

Leek and Lentil Soup

$ ❄

If you don't have homemade chicken broth on hand, use bouillon cubes, powdered bouillon or President's Choice chicken stock concentrate to make the base for this soup. However, if you are on a low-sodium diet, homemade chicken broth is the wise choice. You'll be pleasantly surprised to find how thick this soup becomes with only the small amount of barley called for.

2 leeks, sliced
1 onion, chopped
1 clove garlic, minced
1 cup lentils
¼ cup barley
1 bay leaf
9 cups chicken broth
1 stalk celery, chopped
1 carrot, chopped
1 19-ounce can tomatoes, chopped (including liquid)
Pinch thyme
Pepper to taste

1. Combine leeks, onion and garlic with 3 tablespoons water in a bowl. Cook, covered, in microwave on High for 3 minutes.

2. Put into a soup pot. Stir in lentils, barley, bay leaf and broth.

3. Bring to a boil, reduce heat and simmer, covered, for 30 minutes, stirring occasionally.

4. Add remaining ingredients, cover, and simmer, stirring occasionally, for about 1 hour, or until lentils are tender. Remove bay leaf.

Makes 16 cups. PER 1 CUP SERVING: *Calories: 92, Protein: 7.2 g, Carbohydrates: 13.8 g, Fat: 1.1 g, % Cal. from fat: 11*

Chick Pea and Sweet Potato Soup

$ ❄

This soup makes a hearty dinner when combined with a salad and some crusty bread. Sweet potatoes and yams are extremely high in beta carotene, which is considered an important antioxidant.

- 2 large onions, sliced
- 3 cloves garlic, minced
- 1 stalk celery, sliced
- 2 cups peeled and sliced sweet potatoes
- 5 cups chicken broth
- 1 bay leaf
- 1 teaspoon basil
- 1 19-ounce can tomatoes, chopped (including liquid)
- 1 19-ounce can chick peas, drained
- 3 tablespoons soy sauce

1. Place onion, garlic and celery in a bowl with 3 tablespoons water. Cook, covered, in microwave on High for 4 minutes.

2. Place this mixture in soup pot. Stir in sweet potatoes, chicken broth, bay leaf and basil. Bring to a boil. Reduce heat, cover, and simmer for 30 minutes, stirring occasionally.

3. Add tomatoes, chick peas and soy sauce and simmer the soup for another 15 minutes. Remove bay leaf.

Makes 11 cups. PER 1 CUP SERVING: *Calories: 126, Protein: 6.8 g, Carbohydrates: 21.4 g, Fat: 1.8 g, % Cal. from fat: 12*

Microwave Minestrone Soup

◷ ≋ $ ❄

The amino acids in the kidney beans and macaroni complement each other to make this soup a complete protein. This recipe can also be made on the stove.

1 medium onion, sliced
1 clove garlic, minced
1 carrot, sliced
1 stalk celery, sliced
2 tablespoons water
3 cups beef broth
1 cup tomato sauce
1 teaspoon oregano
1 19-ounce can kidney beans, rinsed
½ cup uncooked elbow macaroni
1 zucchini, sliced
1 teaspoon pepper
1 bay leaf

1. Combine onion, garlic, carrot, celery and 2 tablespoons water in 2-quart casserole dish. Cook, covered, in microwave on High for 4 to 5 minutes.

2. Stir in remaining ingredients. Microwave, covered, on High for 18 minutes, stirring after 6 and 12 minutes. Remove bay leaf.

Makes 8 cups. PER 1 CUP SERVING: *Calories: 116, Protein: 6.7 g, Carbohydrates: 21.7 g, Fat: 0.68 g, % Cal. from fat: 5*

Lentil and Rice Soup

◔ $ ❄

The TGTBT Lentil Soup with Curry is my favourite TGTBT soup. I experimented with cumin to see if I could come up with one I like just as much — and here it is! The combination of lentils (I use red lentils) and rice makes this soup a complete protein.

1 medium onion, chopped
1½ cups lentils
½ cup arborio rice*
9 cups chicken broth
1 teaspoon ground cumin
¼ teaspoon pepper
¼ cup chopped fresh parsley

1. Place onion in small bowl with 3 tablespoons water. Cook, covered, in microwave on High for 3 minutes.

2. Place onion in soup pot. Stir in lentils, rice and chicken broth.

3. Bring to a boil, then simmer partially covered for 50 minutes, stirring occasionally. Lentils will become soft and rice will become creamy.

4. Add last three ingredients and simmer another 5 to 10 minutes.

* Arborio is an Italian rice that you can buy in the bulk food section of a health food store and in some supermarkets.

Makes 11 cups. PER 1 CUP SERVING: *Calories: 154, Protein: 12.1 g, Carbohydrates: 23 g, Fat: 1.4 g, % Cal. from fat: 9*

Black Bean Soup

$ ✳

TGTBT soups are a godsend for those of us with busy schedules. They are quick to prepare, filling, and most important, delicious. Here's my homemade version of the bestselling Black Bean Soup.

2 cups black beans
9½ cups chicken broth
2 large onions, diced
2 cloves garlic, minced
2 large stalks celery, sliced
2 large carrots, sliced
3 tablespoons soy sauce
1 teaspoon ground cumin
¼ teaspoon pepper

1. Cover washed beans with cold water and let soak 8 hours or overnight. (Or put washed beans in a saucepan with 4 cups water. Bring to a boil and simmer, covered, for 2 minutes. Turn off heat and let stand, covered, 1 hour.)

2. Drain the soaked beans, place in large saucepan and add the broth. Bring to a boil, then simmer, partially covered, for 2 to 3 hours, or until beans are thoroughly cooked.

3. Sauté onions, garlic, celery and carrots in a ¼ cup water for 5 minutes or until just tender. (Or cook, covered, in microwave on High for 4 minutes.) Drain vegetables, and add to beans.

4. Season soup with soy sauce, cumin and pepper. Simmer partially covered another 30 minutes, stirring occasionally.

5. Purée in batches in blender or food processor. Serve hot.

Makes 12 cups. PER 1 CUP SERVING: *Calories: 158, Protein: 11.4 g, Carbohydrates: 24.9 g, Fat: 1.6 g, % Cal. from fat: 9*

Green Soup

🍴 💲 ❄️

There are many green soup recipes, but I like this one the best. The puréed zucchini gives the soup a lot of body while keeping the calories low. When you add the spinach, you may wonder where it is all going to go, but it quickly cooks into the soup.

- 1 onion, chopped
- 2 stalks celery (including leaves), chopped
- 6 cups chicken broth
- 1 cup split green peas
- 6 cups diced zucchini (about 4 medium)
- 1 bay leaf
- ½ teaspoon basil
- ½ teaspoon pepper
- 1 package fresh spinach, rinsed well and torn into bite-sized pieces

1. Place onion and celery in bowl with a few tablespoons water. Cook, covered, in microwave on High for 3 minutes.

2. Put onion and celery in a soup pot. Stir in 4 cups broth and peas.

3. Bring to a boil, then simmer, covered, for 45 minutes, stirring occasionally.

4. Add zucchini, remaining broth and seasonings. Simmer 10 additional minutes. Remove bay leaf.

6. Purée soup in batches in a blender or food processor, and return to pot.

7. Stir in spinach and cook 5 minutes.

Makes 10 cups. PER 1 CUP SERVING: *Calories: 116, Protein: 10.2 g, Carbohydrates: 17.2 g, Fat: 1.3 g, % Cal. from fat: 10*

PHOTO: Shrimp and Peppers (page 205)

Mushroom Soup with Barley

☑ ✖ $ ❄

I love to make soup with barley; a small amount of this grain thickens any soup beautifully. This easy-to-prepare soup is special enough to serve to company.

3 cloves garlic, minced
1 large onion, chopped
1 cup dry sherry
1 pound fresh mushrooms, sliced
8 cups beef broth
⅔ cup barley
2 tablespoons soy sauce
¼ cup chopped fresh parsley

1. Place garlic and onion in bowl with 3 tablespoons of water. Cook, covered, in microwave on High for 3 minutes.

2. Place garlic and onion in soup pot. Stir in sherry and mushrooms. Bring to a boil and simmer, covered, for 5 minutes.

3. Add beef broth, barley and soy sauce. Simmer, covered, for 1 hour and 15 minutes, stirring occasionally.

4. Add parsley. Simmer for an additional 10 minutes.

Makes 8 cups. PER 1 CUP SERVING: *Calories: 137, Protein: 6.1 g, Carbohydrates: 18.7 g, Fat: 1.0 g, % Cal. from fat: 7*

PHOTO: *Chicken Mediterranean (page 210)*

Gazpacho

⚔ $

This recipe is best made at the height of summer, when tomatoes are ripe and juicy.

1 English cucumber, peeled, halved lengthwise and seeded
2 large tomatoes, peeled and seeded
1 green pepper, halved
1 medium onion, halved
5 cups tomato juice
1 stalk celery
⅓ cup red wine vinegar
5 cloves garlic, minced
¼ teaspoon Tabasco sauce
¼ teaspoon salt
⅛ to ¼ teaspoon pepper

1. In food processor or blender, combine half the cucumber, 1 tomato, half the green pepper, half the onion and 1 cup of tomato juice. Purée until smooth.

2. Chop remaining vegetables.

3. Pour purée into bowl. Add remaining tomato juice, chopped vegetables, vinegar, garlic and seasonings.

4. Refrigerate, covered, at least 2 hours. Serve cold.

Makes 11 cups. PER 1 CUP SERVING: *Calories: 39, Protein: 1.6 g, Carbohydrates: 9.4 g, Fat: 0.26 g, % Cal. from fat: 5*

Spicy French Dressing

🕐 $

This recipe has less than half the calories of regular French dressing. If you like a bit of kick to your salad dressing, you'll enjoy this recipe. To make it even spicier, add a few extra drops of Tabasco sauce.

½ cup light mayonnaise
2 tablespoons chili sauce
1 teaspoon Worcestershire sauce
1 teaspoon prepared mustard
Few drops Tabasco sauce

1. Combine all ingredients. Mix well.

Makes ⅔ cup. PER 1 TABLESPOON SERVING: *Calories: 38, Protein: 0.13 g, Carbohydrates: 2.6 g, Fat: 3.1 g, % Cal. from fat: 72*

Spicy Tomato Dressing

🕐 $

This recipe has a thinner consistency than the Spicy French Dressing but is every bit as good. I particularly like it on a salad with tuna fish in it.

1 cup tomato or V-8 juice
¼ cup chili sauce
1 tablespoon oil
1 tablespoon lemon juice
2 teaspoons horseradish

1. Combine all ingredients. Mix well and chill.

Makes 1⅓ cups. PER 1 TABLESPOON SERVING: *Calories: 19, Protein: 0.36 g, Carbohydrates: 3.2 g, Fat: 0.66 g, % Cal. from fat: 29*

Yogurt Russian Dressing

◷ $

Some of my clients pour this dressing over chicken and bake it. Sounds good!

½ cup plain low-fat yogurt
½ cup ketchup
1 teaspoon lemon juice
Salt and pepper to taste

1. Combine all ingredients. Mix well.

Makes 1 cup. PER 1 TABLESPOON SERVING: *Calories: 12,
Protein: 0.48 g, Carbohydrates: 2.6 g, Fat: 0.13 g, % Cal. from fat: 9*

Low-Calorie Vinaigrette

◷ $

*Instead of buying antipasto salads, which are often full of fat, mix this
dressing with leftover steamed vegetables. It can also be mixed with
cooked pasta for a cold pasta salad. Typical vinaigrettes contain up to
100 calories per tablespoon. This recipe has only 9!*

1 cup water
⅔ cup balsamic vinegar
2 tablespoons olive oil
2 cloves garlic, minced
1 teaspoon oregano
1 teaspoon basil
1 teaspoon thyme
½ teaspoon pepper
¼ teaspoon salt

1. Combine all ingredients. Chill.

Makes 1 ¾ cups. PER 1 TABLESPOON SERVING: *Calories: 9,
Protein: 0.01 g, Carbohydrates: 0.35 g, Fat: 0.96 g, % Cal. from fat: 85*

Creamy Cucumber Dressing

$

There are a few low-calorie creamy cucumber dressings available. This recipe is as good as the commercial varieties, but more economical.

½ cup light mayonnaise
½ cup pared, seeded and chopped cucumber
1 clove garlic, minced
1 tablespoon minced parsley
1 tablespoon minced green onion
¼ teaspoon salt
Pinch pepper
½ cup plain low-fat yogurt

1. Stir together mayonnaise, cucumber, garlic, parsley, onion, salt and pepper.

2. Fold in yogurt. Chill.

Makes 1½ cups. PER 1 TABLESPOON SERVING: *Calories: 18, Protein: 0.27 g, Carbohydrates: 1.2 g, Fat: 1.3 g, % Cal. from fat: 67*

Yogurt Green Goddess Dressing

☉ $

This dressing makes a good dip for raw vegetables. If you don't have any white wine on hand, substitute rice wine vinegar.

¼ cup light mayonnaise
¼ cup plain low-fat yogurt
2 tablespoons white wine
Dash Worcestershire sauce
1 cup minced fresh parsley
2 tablespoons minced green onion

1. Combine all ingredients. Chill.

Makes 1½ cups. PER 1 TABLESPOON SERVING: *Calories: 10, Protein: 0.18 g, Carbohydrates: 0.73 g, Fat: 0.68 g, % Cal. from fat: 63*

Creamy Greek Dressing

🕐 💲

I like the combination of lemon juice and oregano. If possible use fresh lemon juice.

⅓ cup light mayonnaise
⅓ cup plain low-fat yogurt
¼ cup cold water
¼ cup lemon juice
2 tablespoons minced fresh parsley
2 teaspoons oregano
Salt and pepper to taste

1. Combine all ingredients. Chill.

Makes 1¼ cups. PER 1 TABLESPOON SERVING: *Calories: 15, Protein: 0.28 g, Carbohydrates: 1.2 g, Fat: 1.0 g, % Cal. from fat: 62*

Sesame Oil Vinaigrette

🕐 ✖ 💲

Sesame oil has a distinct flavour and a little goes a long way. This vinaigrette is great on a salad made with Chinese cabbage, bok choy and bean sprouts.

2 cloves garlic, minced
¼ cup rice vinegar
¼ cup water
2 tablespoons sesame oil
2 tablespoons canola oil
2 teaspoons minced fresh ginger
Pinch salt and pepper

1. Combine all ingredients. Chill.

Makes ¾ cup. PER 1 TABLESPOON SERVING: *Calories: 41, Protein: 0.03 g, Carbohydrates: 0.45 g, Fat: 4.5 g, % Cal. from fat: 95*

Poppy Seed Dressing

◷ ✳ $

If you like a dressing on fruit salad, try this one. I also serve it on spinach salad.

⅔ cup light mayonnaise
⅔ cup plain low-fat yogurt
⅓ cup orange juice
1 clove garlic, minced
2½ tablespoons red wine vinegar
2 teaspoons poppy seeds
½ teaspoon pepper

1. Combine all ingredients. Chill.

Makes 1¾ cups. PER 1 TABLESPOON SERVING: *Calories: 23, Protein: 0.39 g, Carbohydrates: 1.8 g, Fat: 1.6 g, % Cal. from fat: 63*

Thousand Island Dressing

◷ $

This dressing is a good alternative to cocktail sauce for a seafood salad.

½ cup light mayonnaise
⅓ cup plain low-fat yogurt
¼ cup cold water
¼ cup ketchup
2 tablespoons relish
2 tablespoons minced fresh parsley
2 tablespoons minced green onion

1. Combine all ingredients. Chill.

Makes 1½ cups. PER 1 TABLESPOON SERVING: *Calories: 22, Protein: 0.32 g, Carbohydrates: 2.2 g, Fat: 1.3 g, % Cal. from fat: 55*

Creamy Italian Dressing

◷ $

Many of my recipes for creamy dressing contain light mayonnaise. If you use TGTBT light mayonnaise, which has only 12 calories per tablespoon instead of 45, as in other brands, you reduce fat calories significantly.

⅓ cup light mayonnaise
⅓ cup red wine or balsamic vinegar
⅓ cup water
1 clove garlic, minced
½ teaspoon oregano
Salt and pepper to taste

1. Combine all ingredients. Chill.

Makes 1 cup. PER 1 TABLESPOON SERVING: *Calories: 15, Protein: 0.01 g, Carbohydrates: 1.0 g, Fat: 1.2 g, % Cal. from fat: 73*

Lemon Caesar Salad Dressing

◷ $

Caesar salads are my favourite. When eating out, I always ask for the dressing on the side. I dip my fork into the thick creamy dressing and then spear a piece of lettuce. This way I get flavour in each mouthful but eat only a minimal amount of dressing.

½ cup light mayonnaise
½ cup fresh lemon juice
1 teaspoon Worcestershire sauce
1 clove garlic, minced
2 tablespoons grated Parmesan cheese
¼ cup minced fresh parsley
Pepper to taste (optional)

1. Combine all ingredients. Chill.

Makes 1¼ cups. PER 1 TABLESPOON SERVING: *Calories: 22, Protein: 0.31 g, Carbohydrates: 1.6 g, Fat: 1.7 g, % Cal. from fat: 67*

Easy Tomato Sauce

⏰ 💲 ❄️

You may want to double this recipe and freeze half. If you don't have time to prepare homemade sauce, President's Choice TGTBT spaghetti sauces taste great and contain approximately 48 calories per ½ cup. The sugar and oil in some commercial sauces bring the calorie count up to 140 per ½ cup.

1 medium onion, chopped
½ green pepper, chopped
½ cup chopped mushrooms
2 cloves garlic, minced
1 28-ounce can tomatoes, chopped (including liquid)
1 5-ounce can tomato paste
1 tablespoon oregano
1 teaspoon basil
1 teaspoon sugar
Salt and pepper to taste

1. Combine onion, green pepper, mushrooms and garlic in bowl with 3 tablespoons water. Cook, covered, in microwave on High (or on top of stove) for 3 minutes. Drain off any water.

2. In a large pot, combine vegetable mixture with remaining ingredients. Bring to a boil, then simmer uncovered for 1 hour or until thickened, stirring occasionally.

Makes approximately 4 cups. PER ½ CUP SERVING: *Calories: 49, Protein: 2.1 g, Carbohydrates: 10.9 g, Fat: 0.5 g, % Cal. from fat: 8*

Fresh Cucumber Sauce

⚔ 💲

At a summer buffet, I like to serve this cucumber sauce with poached salmon. English cucumber is best for this recipe, since the skin is very thin and tender.

1 cup coarsely chopped, unpeeled English cucumber
½ cups plain low-fat yogurt
¼ cup light mayonnaise
1 tablespoon minced green onion
2 teaspoons lemon juice
1 teaspoon prepared mustard
Salt and pepper to taste

1. Place chopped cucumber in colander. Let drain for 30 minutes.

2. Squeeze out any remaining moisture. Combine cucumber with remaining ingredients. Chill.

Makes 1 ¾ cups. PER 2 TABLESPOON SERVING: *Calories: 19, Protein: 0.53 g, Carbohydrates: 1.6 g, Fat: 1.2 g, % Cal. from fat: 57*

Mustard Sauce

🕐 ⚔ 💲

This simple sauce tastes great with poached fish and cold beef or chicken. A smooth Dijon mustard is best for fish, and the grainier ones for beef or chicken.

½ cup plain low-fat yogurt
1 tablespoon dried minced onion
1 tablespoon Dijon mustard

1. Combine all ingredients. Chill.

Makes ½ cup. PER 2 TABLESPOON SERVING: *Calories: 26, Protein: 1.9 g, Carbohydrates: 3.1 g, Fat: 0.74 g, % Cal. from fat: 25*

Sweet and Sour Sauce

⊙ $

*This sauce is a favourite of my clients, and it is a snap to throw together.
I prefer to use fresh garlic and ginger, though the sauce tastes fine when
made with the powdered type.*

½ cup water
¼ cup soy sauce
3 tablespoons vinegar
2 ½ tablespoons Splenda sweetener
½ teaspoon garlic powder *or* 1 clove garlic, minced
¼ teaspoon ground ginger *or* 1 teaspoon minced fresh ginger
¼ teaspoon dry mustard
⅛ teaspoon red pepper flakes
1 tablespoon cornstarch

1. Combine all ingredients, except cornstarch, in a saucepan
and simmer for 1 minute, stirring.

2. Dissolve cornstarch in 2 tablespoons of water and add to the
sauce.

3. Cook, stirring often until the sauce thickens, approximately
2 minutes.

Makes 1 cup. PER ¼ CUP SERVING: *Calories: 22, Protein: 1.6 g,
Carbohydrates: 4.1 g, Fat: 0.008 g, % Cal. from fat: 0*

Black Bean and Brown Rice Salad

✂ $

This salad is filling. A ¾ cup serving with a slice of bread and some raw vegetables is enough for lunch. You can easily double this recipe to make 6 cups.

½ cup black beans, soaked 8 hours or overnight
¾ cup brown rice
1 teaspoon sesame oil
1 tablespoon minced fresh ginger
2 cloves garlic, minced
1 small carrot, finely diced
½ stalk celery, finely diced
2 green onions, finely diced
½ red pepper, finely diced
2 tablespoons soy sauce
1 tablespoon sesame oil
1 tablespoon rice vinegar
2 teaspoons sesame seeds
½ teaspoon honey

1. Drain beans. Put into pot with 2 cups water. Cook, covered, over medium-low heat for 1 hour, or until beans are tender but not mushy. Drain and set aside until cool.

2. In a pot, bring 1½ cups water to a boil. Add rice and simmer, covered, for 40 minutes. Set aside until cool.

3. Spray a non-stick skillet with cooking spray. Add oil and sauté ginger and garlic for 1 minute.

4. Add carrot, celery, onions and red pepper and sauté over low heat for 4 minutes. Add 1 or 2 tablespoons of water if vegetables begin to stick.

5. In a large bowl, combine cooked beans and rice. Stir in vegetable mixture.

6. Combine remaining ingredients in small bowl. Mix well.

7. Add dressing to bean and vegetable mixture and toss.

Makes 4 servings of ¾ cup each. PER SERVING: *Calories: 284, Protein: 9.5 g, Carbohydrates: 47.7 g, Fat: 6.7 g, % Cal. from fat: 21*

Wild Rice and Turkey Salad

Even though wild rice is expensive, it adds enormously to this recipe. If fresh peas are unavailable, diced fresh carrot makes a good substitute.

1   cup chicken broth
1   cup water
¾   cup wild rice
1   cup cooked diced turkey
2   green onions, chopped
½   red pepper, chopped
¼   cup chopped fresh parsley
¼   cup shelled fresh peas
2   tablespoons rice vinegar
1   tablespoon wine vinegar
1½ tablespoons oil
½   teaspoon sugar
½   teaspoon dry mustard
⅛   teaspoon salt
⅛   teaspoon pepper

1. Bring chicken broth and water to a boil. Add rice, cover, and simmer for 40 minutes, or until rice is tender. Let cool.

2. Combine turkey, onions, red pepper, parsley and peas. Stir in rice.

3. Combine remaining ingredients in small bowl. Mix well.

4. Add dressing to rice and turkey mixture. Toss.

Makes 4 servings of 1 cup each. PER SERVING: *Calories: 250, Protein: 18.9 g, Carbohydrates: 26.2 g, Fat: 7.9 g, % Cal. from fat: 28*

Roasted Eggplant and Pepper Salad

✖

A couple of years ago, I created a line of food for a Toronto gourmet shop. This salad was the most popular of all.

2 medium eggplants (about 3 pounds), unpeeled, cubed
1 red pepper
1 yellow pepper
1 cup cherry tomatoes, halved
1 cup coarsely chopped fresh parsley
3 tablespoons balsamic vinegar
1 tablespoon oregano
1 ½ teaspoons basil
Dash salt and pepper

1. Spray two cookie sheets with cooking spray. Lay cubed eggplant on sheets and spray very lightly with cooking spray. Bake at 425°F for 20 to 25 minutes, turning after 10 minutes.

2. Place whole peppers on electric stove element turned to high. When peppers start to blacken, turn and continue to grill until all sides are done. Let cool, then slice peppers into strips, removing stem and seeds. (If you have a gas stove, cut peppers into one-inch cubes and bake on cookie sheets with eggplant.)

3. In a large bowl, combine eggplant and peppers with remaining ingredients. Chill.

Makes 6 servings of 1¼ cup each. PER SERVING: *Calories: 24, Protein: 0.98 g, Carbohydrates: 5.7 g, Fat: 0.17 g, % Cal. from fat: 6*

Asparagus Salad

✖

I tasted this salad at Vincent's, a great restaurant in Phoenix, Arizona. It was one of the choices on the "alternative menu" and was so delicious that I have tried to duplicate it.

1   small red pepper
1   small yellow pepper
1   pound raw asparagus, cut in ½-inch pieces
⅓   cup diced red onion
1   small head Bibb lettuce
¼   cup sherry or rice vinegar
2   teaspoons oil
1   teaspoon honey
½   teaspoon basil

1. Place whole peppers on electric stove element turned to high. When peppers start to blacken, turn and continue to cook until all sides are done. Let cool. (If you have a gas stove, bake peppers on a cookie sheet sprayed with cooking spray at 425°F, for 15 to 20 minutes. Turn after 7 or 8 minutes.)

2. Slice peppers into thin strips, removing stems and seeds. Place in bowl.

3. Add asparagus, onion and half the lettuce, torn into bite-sized pieces.

4. In a small bowl combine remaining ingredients. Mix well.

5. Pour dressing over vegetables and toss well.

6. Line individual salad plates with remaining lettuce leaves and spoon salad on top.

Makes 4 servings. PER SERVING: *Calories: 90, Protein: 4.6 g, Carbohydrates: 10.6 g, Fat: 2.7 g, % Cal. from fat: 29*

Tabbouleh

$

Tabbouleh is a great summer salad with a hot or cold meal. It's simple to make and will keep four or five days.

2　cups water
1　cup bulgur (or cracked wheat)
⅓　cup lemon juice
2　cloves garlic, minced
¼　teaspoon salt
¼　teaspoon pepper
2　large tomatoes, chopped
1　large red onion, chopped
1　cup chopped fresh parsley

1. Combine water and bulgur in a large bowl and let stand until all water is absorbed, approximately 45 minutes.

2. Combine lemon juice, garlic, salt and pepper. Add to bulgur and mix well.

3. Add remaining ingredients and mix well.

Makes 6 servings of 1 cup each. PER SERVING: *Calories: 104, Protein: 3.9 g, Carbohydrates: 23.7 g, Fat: 0.48 g, % Cal. from fat: 4*

New Potato and Dill Salad

✕ $

This versatile salad is delicious served warm, cold or at room temperature.

1　pound new potatoes (about 12 to 14), quartered
2　green onions, sliced
1　small red pepper, diced
2　tablespoons chopped fresh dill
1½　tablespoons olive oil
1½　tablespoons red wine vinegar
¼　teaspoon salt
¼　teaspoon pepper

1. Bring 2 cups water to a boil. Add potatoes and cook, partially covered, over medium heat for 15 to 18 minutes, or until tender. Drain.

2. Combine remaining ingredients in a bowl. Add warm potatoes and toss gently.

Makes 4 servings of approximately ¾ cup each. PER SERVING: *Calories: 173, Protein: 3.1 g, Carbohydrates: 29.7 g, Fat: 5.2 g, % Cal. from fat: 26*

Tofu Salad with Green Beans and Mushrooms

$

Tofu has little taste of its own, but it takes on the flavour of whatever it is cooked with. For those with a lactose intolerance, it makes a good alternative to milk and cheese, since it has a significant calcium content.

1   pound green beans, cut into 1½-inch pieces
½   pound fresh mushrooms, sliced
¼   cup soy sauce
8   ounces tofu, cubed
2   green onions, sliced

1. Steam green beans until tender.

2. Spray a non-stick skillet with cooking spray. Lightly sauté mushrooms. Drain liquid from pan. Stir in 1 tablespoon soy sauce. Remove mushrooms from pan.

3. Respray skillet. Add tofu and 2 tablespoons of soya sauce. Sauté until lightly browned.

4. Combine mushrooms, green beans and tofu in a bowl with green onions. Add remaining tablespoon soy sauce and mix gently. Chill.

Makes 4 servings. PER SERVING: *Calories: 106, Protein: 8.9 g, Carbohydrates: 14.2 g, Fat: 3.1 g, % Cal. from fat: 23*

Farmer's Salad

$

A farmer's salad is usually made with sour cream. In this recipe, cottage cheese, Worcestershire sauce and mustard provide the tang instead. This salad makes a great lunch for two.

1½ cups low-fat (1%) cottage cheese
1 tablespoon Worcestershire sauce
1 teaspoon Dijon mustard
2 stalks celery, chopped
1 green pepper, diced
1 red pepper, diced
2 carrots, grated
4 radishes, sliced
Salt and pepper to taste (optional)

1. Combine cottage cheese, Worcestershire sauce and mustard. Mix well.

2. Add remaining ingredients and toss.

Makes 2 servings. PER SERVING: *Calories: 192, Protein: 23 g, Carbohydrates: 20.2 g, Fat: 2.2 g, % Cal. from fat: 10*

Green Bean Salad with Mustard and Dill

⊘ ✕ $

Make this salad when green beans are at their peak — sweet and crisp.

1 pound green beans, cut into 1 ½-inch pieces
½ cup chopped fresh dill
6 green onions, chopped
1 teaspoon oil
3 tablespoons balsamic vinegar
2 tablespoons Dijon mustard
¼ teaspoon salt
¼ teaspoon pepper

1. Steam green beans until just tender. Add dill and onions.

2. Whisk together remaining ingredients in small bowl.

3. Add dressing to bean mixture and toss. Chill.

Makes 5 servings of 1 cup each. PER SERVING: *Calories: 44, Protein: 2.0g, Carbohydrates: 7.7 g, Fat: 1.3 g, % Cal. from fat: 23*

Chinese Cabbage and Bean Sprout Salad

◷ ✗ $

Chinese cabbage is now available at many supermarkets and small vegetable markets in Canada's larger cities. This salad is special enough for company and will not wilt if served on a buffet.

4 cups thinly sliced Chinese cabbage
4 cups bean sprouts
2 green onions, sliced
½ red pepper, sliced
3 tablespoons soy sauce
3 tablespoons lemon juice
1 tablespoon sesame oil
1 teaspoon honey
1 teaspoon minced fresh ginger

1. In a large bowl, combine cabbage, sprouts, onion and red pepper.

2. In a small bowl, whisk together remaining ingredients.

3. Pour dressing over vegetables. Toss.

Makes 4 servings. PER SERVING: *Calories: 92, Protein: 5.2 g, Carbohydrates: 12.9 g, Fat: 3.7 g, % Cal. from fat: 32*

Black Bean and Coriander Salad

❌ 💲

This salad tastes best served warm or at room temperature. If you dislike coriander, the dish is just as good with fresh parsley.

 1 cup black beans, soaked for 8 hours or overnight
 1 cup chicken broth
 ½ cup diced red onion
 2 cloves garlic, minced
 2 tablespoons balsamic vinegar
 1 tablespoon olive oil
 ⅛ teaspoon red pepper flakes
10 cherry tomatoes, halved
 ½ cup chopped fresh coriander

1. Drain the beans, reserving the liquid. Measure 1½ cups of the reserved liquid, adding water if necessary.

2. Place beans, liquid and chicken broth in pot. Bring to a boil, then simmer, covered, for 1 hour, or until beans are tender but not mushy. Drain.

3. Combine onion, garlic, vinegar, oil and red pepper flakes. Add to warm beans and toss.

4. Let sit for 10 minutes to allow flavours to develop.

5. Add cherry tomatoes and coriander. Toss gently.

Makes 4 servings of ¾ cup each. PER SERVING: *Calories: 225, Protein: 12.5 g, Carbohydrates: 35 g, Fat: 4.6 g, % Cal. from fat: 18*

Millet Salad

❌

This salad will keep four or five days in the refrigerator. Use white wine vinegar instead of red wine vinegar; the red stains the millet and vegetable mixture.

1 cup millet
½ pound snow peas, sliced
3 medium carrots, julienned
1 medium zucchini, julienned
1 10-ounce can water chestnuts, drained and sliced
¼ cup white wine vinegar
2 tablespoons lemon juice
2 tablespoons minced fresh ginger
1 tablespoon oil
1 clove garlic, minced
Dash salt and pepper

1. Cook millet in 3 cups water for 20 to 25 minutes, or until all water is absorbed.

2. Combine snow peas, carrots, zucchini and water chestnuts with cooked millet.

3. Whisk together remaining ingredients in small bowl, then toss with millet and vegetable mixture. Refrigerate.

Makes 11 servings of 1 cup each. PER SERVING: *Calories: 112, Protein: 3.2 g, Carbohydrates: 20.5 g, Fat: 2.1 g, % Cal. from fat: 17*

Yogurt Cucumber Salad

☻ $

If you like a creamy dressing for cucumbers, try this recipe. I love it.

½ cup plain low-fat yogurt
2 tablespoons lemon juice
1 teaspoon sugar
½ teaspoon salt
2 English cucumbers, thinly sliced

1. Combine yogurt, lemon juice, sugar and salt.

2. Pour over cucumber slices and toss. Chill.

Makes 6 servings of 1 cup each. PER SERVING: *Calories: 25, Protein: 1.3 g, Carbohydrates: 4.6 g, Fat: 0.38 g, % Cal. from fat: 13*

Marinated Squid Salad

✂ $

Although it is considered a gourmet food, squid is inexpensive and, now that seafood shops have cleaned squid available, easy to use.

3   cloves garlic, minced
1   tablespoon lemon juice
2   teaspoons olive oil
1   teaspoon Dijon mustard
½   teaspoon pepper
⅛   teaspoon dried basil
Dash cayenne
1   pound cleaned squid, sliced into rings
¼   red onion, thinly sliced
1   green pepper, cut in chunks
1   tablespoon chopped parsley
2   tomatoes, chopped

1. In skillet combine garlic, lemon juice, oil, mustard, pepper, basil and cayenne. Bring to boil.

2. Add squid. Sauté for 1 minute, or until squid turns white. Remove from heat and transfer to bowl.

3. Stir in onion and green pepper. Cover and refrigerate 2 hours or overnight.

4. Before serving, add parsley and tomatoes and toss.

Makes 4 appetizers or 2 main-course servings. PER APPETIZER SERVING: *Calories: 152, Protein: 18.7 g, Carbohydrates: 9.6 g, Fat: 4.1 g, % Cal. from fat: 25*

Oriental Marinated Cucumber Salad

◷ $

This salad is so easy to make that as soon as I use up one batch I make another. I serve it as an accompaniment to a sandwich for lunch, as a salad with dinner or as a mid-afternoon snack.

3 tablespoons rice or white vinegar
3 tablespoons soy sauce
2 teaspoons sugar
1 teaspoon ground ginger
1 English cucumber, thinly sliced
2 green onions, sliced

1. Combine vinegar, soy sauce, sugar and ginger.

2. In a separate bowl, combine cucumber and green onions.

3. Pour dressing on top. Mix well. Chill.

Makes 5 servings of 1 cup each. PER SERVING: *Calories: 21, Protein: 1.2 g, Carbohydrates: 4.6 g, Fat: 0.05 g, % Cal. from fat: 2*

Barbie's Special Salad

✂

This is a nice change from a tossed salad. I serve it as a first course, and every time I do, someone asks for the recipe.

1 tablespoon rice vinegar
1 teaspoon soy sauce
1 teaspoon honey
½ teaspoon ground ginger
2 cups English cucumber, thinly sliced
1 head Boston lettuce, torn into pieces
1 cup snow peas, sliced
5 radishes, thinly sliced
1 tablespoon sesame oil
2 teaspoons lemon juice

1. Combine vinegar, soy sauce, honey and ginger in a jar. Shake well.

2. Place cucumber in a bowl and pour dressing on top. Toss well.

3. Combine lettuce, snow peas and radishes in a large bowl.

4. Combine oil and lemon juice in a cup. Mix well, then pour over lettuce mixture.

5. Add cucumber mixture and toss.

Makes 4 small or 2 large servings. PER SMALL SERVING: *Calories: 65, Protein: 1.8 g, Carbohydrates: 7.3 g, Fat: 3.6 g, % Cal. from fat: 47*

Bean and Cheese Casserole

⊙ $ ❄

This recipe is particularly easy if you can buy TGTBT Great Northern or Precooked 7 Bean Mix (they come in a jar and are ready to use). A combination of canned kidney beans, chick peas or lentils could be substituted.

1 large onion, sliced
2 cloves garlic, minced
2 cups sliced assorted fresh vegetables (zucchini, celery, mushrooms, carrots, broccoli)
2 cups tomato sauce
2 teaspoons soy sauce
½ teaspoon thyme
½ teaspoon pepper
4 cups cooked beans, rinsed and drained
4 ounces low-fat cheese, grated

1. In large pot, combine all ingredients except beans and cheese. Cook, uncovered, over medium heat for 10 to 15 minutes, stirring frequently.

2. Add beans and cook another 8 minutes. Pour into casserole dish.

3. Sprinkle with cheese. Broil for 8 minutes, or until brown and bubbly.

Makes 4 servings. PER SERVING: *Calories: 398, Protein: 25.8 g, Carbohydrates: 64 g, Fat: 6.2 g, % Cal. from fat: 14*

Lentils and Herbed Rice

◷ ≋ $ ❄

Lentils are a convenient legume to prepare since they do not require any soaking. This recipe can also be made on top of the stove. I think it tastes best made with low-fat Lappi or Danbo cheese.

2⅔ cups water
1 cup chopped onion
¾ cup lentils
½ cup brown rice
1 beef bouillon cube
½ teaspoon basil
½ teaspoon oregano
¼ teaspoon thyme
⅛ teaspoon garlic powder
3 ounces low-fat cheese, shredded

1. In a 2-quart casserole dish, combine all ingredients except cheese. Cover tightly and cook in microwave on High for 15 minutes.

2. Stir well. Microwave, covered, on Medium-Low for 30 minutes. If all water is not absorbed and lentils and rice are not tender, cook an additional 5 to 10 minutes.

3. Stir cheese thoroughly into mixture.

Makes 4 servings of 1 cup each. PER SERVING: *Calories: 283, Protein: 18.6 g, Carbohydrates: 42.2 g, Fat: 4.8 g, % Cal. from fat: 15*

Lentil Stew

$ ❄

Served on a bed of rice, this dish makes an economical, filling supper. If you prefer a thicker stew, cook uncovered for the last 10 to 15 minutes.

1 large onion, chopped
2 cloves garlic, minced
2 zucchini, sliced
1 green pepper, sliced
1 red pepper, sliced
1 eggplant, unpeeled, cut into cubes
1 tablespoon chili powder
1 teaspoon cumin
1 teaspoon oregano
½ teaspoon salt
¼ teaspoon pepper
1 28-ounce can tomatoes, chopped (including liquid)
2 cups vegetable broth or water
1¼ cups lentils

1. Combine onion and garlic in a bowl with 3 tablespoons water. Cook, covered, in microwave on High for 2 minutes.

2. Place, with all the liquid, in a large pot. Stir in zucchini, peppers and eggplant, and cook over medium heat for 5 minutes, stirring occasionally.

3. Stir in seasonings and cook another 5 minutes, stirring occasionally.

4. Add tomatoes, broth and lentils. Bring to a boil. Reduce heat to medium-low and cook, covered, for 40 minutes.

Makes 6 servings of 2 cups each. PER SERVING: *Calories: 190, Protein: 13.8 g, Carbohydrates: 35 g, Fat: 0.88 g, % Cal. from fat: 4*

Black Bean Chili

$ ❄

Most people like chili. It's real comfort food.

1   cup black beans, soaked 8 hours or overnight
1   large onion, chopped
1   clove garlic, minced
1½ tablespoons chili powder
1   teaspoon basil
1   teaspoon ground cumin
2   stalks celery, chopped
1   green pepper, chopped
1   28-ounce can tomatoes, chopped (including liquid)
1   5-ounce can tomato paste
1   teaspoon soy sauce

1. In a pot, cover beans with water. Bring to a boil. Simmer, covered, 1 hour, or until softened. Drain and set aside.

2. Combine onion and garlic with 3 tablespoons water. Cook, covered, in microwave on High for 3 minutes.

3. Put onion and garlic and any remaining water into a large pot over medium heat. Add spices and sauté 1 minute.

4. Add celery and sauté for 5 minutes. Add green pepper and sauté another 5 minutes.

5. Add tomatoes, tomato paste and soy sauce, and cook 5 minutes, stirring frequently.

6. Add cooked beans. Cook partially covered over medium-low heat 30 minutes, stirring frequently.

Makes 4 servings of 1¾ cups each. PER SERVING: *Calories: 259, Protein: 14.6 g, Carbohydrates: 50.8 g, Fat: 1.6 g, % Cal. from fat: 5*

Tofu Chili

🕐 $ ❄

If you want to disguise tofu, try this recipe. My clients tell me that their families adore it and are happy to know they are eating something healthy.

1 pound tofu
1 green pepper, diced
2 medium onions, diced
1 stalk celery, sliced
1 carrot, sliced
1 clove garlic, minced
1 28-ounce can plum tomatoes, chopped (including liquid)
1 19-ounce can kidney beans, undrained
1 6-ounce can tomato paste
½ teaspoon cayenne pepper (or to taste)
½ teaspoon oregano
½ teaspoon basil
Pepper to taste (optional)

1. Place tofu in strainer and press out excess water.

2. Place green pepper, onion, celery, carrot and garlic in a bowl with 3 tablespoons of water. Cover and cook in microwave on High for 3 to 4 minutes. Drain.

3. In large pot add remaining ingredients and vegetable mixture.

4. Stir in drained tofu. Bring to a boil, then simmer, covered, for 1 hour, stirring occasionally.

Makes 6 servings of 1 ½ cups each. PER SERVING: *Calories: 217, Protein: 14.4 g, Carbohydrates: 33.4 g, Fat: 4.6 g, % Cal. from fat: 18*

Szechwan Tofu and Broccoli

🕐 💲

This dish is so filling that you may find it feeds more than two people. Pressed tofu is found in health food stores and in the TGTBT line; it's better than unpressed tofu for stir-frying, since it is denser and doesn't fall apart.

2   teaspoons oil
2   green onions, sliced
1   green pepper, sliced
2   cloves garlic, minced
¼   teaspoon red pepper flakes
1   bunch broccoli, cut into pieces including (trimmed) stems
½   cup vegetable broth or water
2   tablespoons soy sauce
1   tablespoon cornstarch
1   pound pressed tofu, cubed

1. Heat oil in skillet over high heat. Add green onions, green pepper, garlic and red pepper flakes. Stir-fry for 4 to 5 seconds.

2. Add broccoli and stir-fry for 3 minutes.

3. Combine broth, soy sauce and cornstarch in a small bowl. Add cornstarch mixture to the skillet. Cook, stirring frequently, for 2 minutes, or until thickened.

4. Add tofu and stir-fry gently until tofu is heated through.

Makes 2 servings. PER SERVING: *Calories: 369, Protein: 42.9 g, Carbohydrates: 33.7 g, Fat: 9.0 g, % Cal. from fat: 21*

Tofu Quiche

$ ❄

This recipe makes a good lunch entree, or a light supper when served with bread and a salad. I find low-fat Danbo cheese works very well because its sharp taste contrasts with the tofu.

1 pound tofu
3 eggs
½ cup skim milk
1½ tablespoons cornstarch
1 teaspoon Worcestershire sauce
½ teaspoon salt
½ teaspoon pepper
3 green onions, chopped
1 10-ounce package frozen spinach, cooked and drained
4 ounces low-fat cheese, shredded

1. Combine tofu, eggs, milk, cornstarch, Worcestershire sauce, salt and pepper in a food processor or blender and blend until smooth.

2. Mix onions, spinach and cheese into tofu mixture. Pour into oven-proof pie plate sprayed with cooking spray.

3. Bake at 325°F for 45 minutes.

Makes 4 servings. PER SERVING: *Calories: 243, Protein: 23.8 g, Carbohydrates: 12.1 g, Fat: 11.1 g, % Cal. from fat: 41*

Tofu Broccoli Spaghetti

$ ❄

The combination of pasta, tofu, broccoli and cheese makes this a complete meal. It freezes well and can be heated in the microwave for a quick, satisfying dinner. Any kind of pasta noodle can be used.

½ pound pasta
1 bunch broccoli, cut into pieces, including stems
1 pound tofu
1½ cups tomato sauce
4 ounces low-fat mozzarella, shredded

1. Cook pasta according to package instructions. Drain.

2. Place broccoli in a bowl with 3 tablespoons of water. Cover and cook in microwave on High for 3 minutes.

3. Mash tofu in a strainer to remove water.

4. Combine pasta, broccoli, tofu, tomato sauce and cheese in baking dish. Bake at 350°F for 25 minutes.

Makes 4 servings. PER SERVING: *Calories: 430, Protein: 28.1 g, Carbohydrates: 57.7 g, Fat: 11.5 g, % Cal. from fat: 23*

Tofu Cacciatore

◷ $ ❄

This dish tastes even better if prepared the day before, to give the tofu time to absorb the tomato flavour. Serve over pasta or brown rice.

1 pound tofu, cut into ½-inch cubes
1 cup tomato sauce
1 zucchini, sliced
½ pound fresh mushrooms, sliced
½ green pepper, sliced
½ large onion, sliced
2 cloves garlic, minced

PHOTO: *Company Chicken (page 209);
Beef Kabobs (page 220)*

1. Spray a skillet with cooking spray and heat over medium heat. Add tofu and brown on all sides.

2. Mix remaining ingredients in baking dish. Stir in tofu.

3. Bake at 350°F for 25 to 30 minutes.

Makes 2 very hearty servings. PER SERVING: *Calories: 280, Protein: 24.2 g, Carbohydrates: 27.8 g, Fat: 11.8 g, % Cal. from fat: 34*

Oven-Cooked Barbecue Tofu

$ ❄

If you buy very firm tofu, for example the TGTBT tofu, this dish can be barbecued. Slice the tofu in half and marinate it in TGTBT barbecue sauce, or marinate with the sauce recipe given below. Barbecue for 4 to 5 minutes per side.

1½ pounds pressed tofu, cut into strips
Barbecue Sauce:
1 small onion, chopped
1 cup tomato sauce
5 tablespoons soy sauce
2 tablespoons molasses
2 tablespoons white vinegar
1 tablespoon Worcestershire sauce

1. Put onion in small bowl with 2 tablespoons water. Cook, covered, in microwave on High for 2 minutes. Drain.

2. Heat a non-stick skillet sprayed with cooking spray. Add onion and remaining sauce ingredients and simmer for 10 minutes, stirring occasionally.

3. Spread small amount of sauce on cookie sheet sprayed with cooking spray. Lay tofu strips on top of sauce, then pour remaining sauce over strips, completely covering each strip. Marinate 30 minutes.

4. Bake at 350°F for 35 minutes.

Makes 4 servings. PER SERVING: *Calories: 254, Protein: 28.8 g, Carbohydrates: 29.6 g, Fat: 2.8 g, % Cal. from fat: 10*

PHOTO: *Barbecued Vegetable Packages (page 232); Skillet Squash (page 229)*

Pasta Primavera

$ ❄

I use penne or rigatoni pasta in this recipe, since the little tubes hold the sauce. Any combination of vegetables can be used. If you have others on hand, try them. The TGTBT Salsa Spaghetti Sauce is a great accompaniment to this dish, as is the tomato sauce recipe in this book.

- ½ pound pasta (penne or rigatoni are best)
- 1 cup cauliflower florets
- 1 cup broccoli florets
- 2 medium zucchini, sliced
- ½ pound fresh mushrooms, sliced
- 1 green pepper, cut into strips
- 1 red pepper, cut into strips
- 2 cups tomato sauce

1. Cook pasta according to package instructions. Drain and return to pot.

2. While cooking pasta, combine all vegetables in large bowl with ½ cup water. Cook, covered, in microwave on High for 6 minutes, stirring once after 3 minutes.

3. Add vegetables and tomato sauce to pasta in pot. Toss well. Heat through.

Makes 4 servings. PER SERVING: *Calories: 307, Protein: 13.5 g, Carbohydrates: 63.3 g, Fat: 1.7 g, % Cal. from fat: 5*

Splendido Pizza with Grilled Vegetables

President's Choice Splendido Flatbread makes a wonderful crust for a pizza. If this product is unavailable, choose a pizza dough without a lot of oil. Many supermarkets and bakery shops now carry both white and whole wheat varieties.

1 green pepper
1 red pepper
1 zucchini, sliced lengthwise
½ cup tomato sauce
1 Splendido Flatbread or 1-pound pizza crust
8 ounces low-fat mozzarella, shredded
1 tablespoon oregano
1 teaspoon basil

1. To grill peppers and zucchini, turn three electric stove elements to high. Place both peppers on one element. When skin starts to blacken, turn peppers; continue to cook, turning until all sides are done. Meanwhile, place zucchini strips on other two burners. Turn when they start to blacken. (If using a gas stove, seed and core peppers and cut into strips. Place peppers and zucchini on cookie sheet sprayed with cooking spray. Bake at 425°F for 15 to 20 minutes.)

2. Pour tomato sauce over pizza crust. Sprinkle cheese on top.

3. Slice peppers and zucchini into small strips and lay over cheese. Sprinkle with oregano and basil.

6. Bake at 425°F for 10 to 12 minutes.

Makes 4 main-course or 8 appetizer servings. PER APPETIZER SERVING: *Calories: 222, Protein: 12.7 g, Carbohydrates: 27.6 g, Fat: 6.2 g, % Cal. from fat: 26*

Grilled Vegetable Lasagna

Grilling vegetables is an extra step that is well worth the effort. It gives this dish a special flavour and makes it a treat for your guests.

1   red pepper
1   yellow pepper
2   zucchini, sliced lengthwise
1   eggplant, unpeeled, sliced
¾   pound lasagna noodles (¾ of 500-gram package)
¾   pound low-fat mozzarella, shredded
2   cups tomato sauce

1. Heat three electric stove elements to high. Place both peppers on one element and cook until they start to blacken. Turn and repeat with other sides. Lay zucchini slices on the two other elements and turn when they start to blacken. When cool, slice and set aside. (If using a gas stove, seed and core peppers and cut into strips. Place peppers and zucchini with eggplant on cookie sheet sprayed with cooking spray. Bake at 425°F for 15 to 20 minutes.)

2. Lay eggplant slices on cookie sheet sprayed with cooking spray. Bake at 425°F for 15 to 20 minutes.

3. In large pot of boiling water, cook lasagna noodles until al dente. Drain. Return to pot and cover with cold water.

4. In a 13-x-9 inch baking dish, spread a small amount of sauce. Cover with a layer of lasagna noodles. Spread eggplant slices over noodles and sprinkle with a third of the cheese. Lay another layer of noodles over cheese and spread sauce over noodles. Spread zucchini and pepper slices over noodles and sprinkle with another third of the cheese. Pour remaining sauce over cheese and sprinkle with the last third of the cheese.

5. Bake at 350°F for 35 minutes, or until bubbly. Let rest 15 minutes before slicing.

Makes 8 servings. PER SERVING: *Calories: 301, Protein: 17.6 g, Carbohydrates: 40.3 g , Fat: 7.8 g, % Cal. from fat: 23*

Halibut in Wine Sauce

🕐 🍴

Other firm-fleshed fish work well in this recipe, which is similar in preparation to Company Chicken. The three colourful peppers make it a very attractive dish.

2 medium onions, sliced
4 halibut steaks (about 1½ pounds total)
1 green pepper, sliced
1 red pepper, sliced
1 yellow pepper, sliced
¾ cup chopped fresh parsley
¼ cup dry white wine
½ cup coarsely chopped fresh dill
3 tablespoons lemon juice
⅛ teaspoon pepper

1. Arrange onion slices in baking dish sprayed with cooking spray. Place fish on top.

2. Combine peppers and parsley and arrange over fish.

3. Combine last four ingredients and pour over all. Bake, covered, at 400°F for 20 minutes.

Makes 4 servings. PER SERVING: *Calories: 253, Protein: 36.7 g, Carbohydrates: 9.1 g, Fat: 4.1 g, % Cal. from fat: 15*

Grilled Tuna

⊙

The meaty flesh of tuna appeals to many people. But make sure not to over-cook it, or it will taste dry. This dish is also great when swordfish is used.

2 tablespoons lemon juice
2 tablespoons dry white wine
1 teaspoon olive oil
1 teaspoon Worcestershire sauce
Fresh black pepper
4 tuna steaks (about 1½ pounds total)

1. Combine all ingredients except tuna in small bowl.

2. Pour marinade over fish and marinate for 1 hour.

3. Broil or barbecue for 2 to 4 minutes per side, depending on thickness of fish.

Makes 4 servings. PER SERVING: *Calories: 263, Protein: 39.8 g, Carbohydrates: 0.82 g, Fat: 9.4 g, % Cal. from fat: 34*

Sautéed Orange Roughy

⊙ ✗

Orange Roughy is imported all the way from New Zealand. It comes to Canada frozen, so if you buy it thawed (or "fresh"), it should be cooked the same day and not be refrozen.

1 cup dry white wine
1 cup chopped mushrooms
2 cloves garlic, minced
2 tablespoons chopped fresh dill
4 orange roughy fillets (about 1½ pounds total)

1. Place first four ingredients in a large skillet. Bring to a boil.

2. Add fish fillets and simmer for 8 to 10 minutes, or until fish flakes when tested with a fork.

Makes 4 servings. PER SERVING: *Calories: 233, Protein: 35.9 g, Carbohydrates: 1.7 g, Fat: 3.9 g, % Cal. from fat: 15*

Orange Roughy in Oriental Sauce

When you are in a rush, cook this in the microwave. I also enjoy it cold for lunch the next day with a salad.

½ cup soy sauce
3 tablespoons lemon juice
2 cloves garlic, minced
4 orange roughy fillets (about 1½ pounds total)

1. Combine first three ingredients in small bowl.

2. Pour over fish and marinate at least 20 minutes.

3. Remove fish, reserving marinade. Broil or barbecue for 3 to 4 minutes per side, basting with remaining marinade.

Makes 4 servings. PER SERVING: *Calories: 215, Protein: 38.7 g, Carbohydrates: 4.4 g, Fat: 3.9 g, % Cal. from fat: 17*

Salmon Teriyaki

◎ ✂

Salmon is oilier than most fish but is recommended for its abundance of omega-3 fatty acids, which help lower cholesterol. Since its flesh is firm, it cooks well on the barbecue.

¼ cup soy sauce
2 cloves garlic, minced
1 tablespoon minced fresh ginger
1 tablespoon lemon juice
1 teaspoon honey
4 salmon fillets (about 1 pound total)

1. Combine all ingredients except salmon in a small bowl.

2. Pour marinade over fish and marinate at least 30 minutes.

3. Bake fish at 350°F for 12 minutes, or until it just flakes with a fork. (Alternatively, broil or barbecue, basting with marinade, for 3 to 4 minutes on each side.)

Makes 4 servings. PER SERVING: *Calories: 182, Protein: 24.2 g, Carbohydrates: 4 g, Fat: 7.2 g, % Cal. from fat: 37*

Spanish-Style Cod

$ ≋

I find this recipe spicy enough, but some of my clients who love really spicy food put in more green chilies. If you don't have any chilies on hand, use ¼ teaspoon red pepper flakes. This dish can be cooked in a microwave. Place in a baking dish covered with plastic wrap (turn back one corner to allow steam to escape). Cook on High for 6 to 7 minutes, turning after the first 3 minutes.

4 cod fillets (about 1½ pounds total)
Pepper to taste
1 cup chopped onion
¼ cup diced green chilies
3 tomatoes, chopped
¾ cup chopped parsley
3 tablespoons lime juice
1 teaspoon oregano
½ teaspoon sugar
Lime wedges

1. Sprinkle cod with pepper and place in baking dish sprayed with cooking spray.

2. Combine remaining ingredients, except lime wedges, in a small bowl. Mix well and pour over cod.

3. Bake at 400°F for 12 minutes. Serve with lime wedges.

Makes 4 servings. PER SERVING: *Calories: 185, Protein: 32.2 g, Carbohydrates: 10.5 g, Fat: 1.5 g, % Cal. from fat: 7*

Marlin, Pepper and Mushroom Medley

✄

I discovered marlin quite by accident when I thought I was buying swordfish. It's similar in taste and texture and won't fall apart when you stir-fry it.

1 pound marlin, cut into 1-inch strips
1 green pepper, sliced
1 red pepper, sliced
½ pound fresh mushrooms, sliced
1 medium onion, sliced
3 tablespoons lemon juice
3 tablespoons soy sauce

1. Spray a large non-stick skillet or wok with cooking spray. Cook fish strips over medium-high heat for 2 minutes, browning each side.

2. Add peppers, mushrooms and onion, and sauté for 3 to 4 minutes, or until vegetables soften.

3. Stir in lemon juice and soy sauce. Heat through, stirring mixture gently.

Makes 4 servings. PER SERVING: *Calories: 191, Protein: 26.8 g, Carbohydrates: 8.8 g, Fat: 5.4 g, % Cal. from fat: 26*

Garlic Scallops

✄ ◷

This dish, which can be prepared from start to finish in 15 minutes, is delicious tossed with pasta. For extra flavour, use President's Choice Olive Oil with Garlic Essence.

1 pound scallops
3 cloves garlic, minced
2 tablespoons lemon juice
1 tablespoon olive oil

¼ teaspoon salt
⅛ teaspoon pepper

1. Place scallops in baking dish sprayed with cooking spray. Heat broiler.

2. Combine remaining ingredients and toss with scallops.

3. Broil 5 inches from heat for 4 to 5 minutes. Turn scallops and broil for another 4 to 5 minutes.

Makes 4 servings. PER SERVING: *Calories: 135, Protein: 19.2 g, Carbohydrates: 4.0 g, Fat: 4.2 g, % Cal. from fat: 29*

Lemon-Baked Snapper

≋

This dish can be cooked in the microwave. Cover the baking dish with plastic wrap, turning back one corner to allow steam to escape.

1 cup chopped onion
2 tomatoes, chopped
1 cup chopped celery
4 snapper fillets (about 1 ½ pounds total)
½ cup chopped fresh parsley
2 tablespoons Worcestershire sauce
2 tablespoons lemon juice
Lemon wedges

1. Combine ½ cup onion with tomatoes and celery.

2. Sprinkle over bottom of baking dish sprayed with cooking spray.

3. Place fish fillets over vegetables.

4. Combine parsley, Worcestershire sauce, lemon juice and remaining onion. Spoon over fish.

5. Bake, uncovered, at 400°F for 12 to 15 minutes. Serve with lemon wedges.

Makes 4 servings. PER SERVING: *Calories: 212, Protein: 36.9 g, Carbohydrates: 9.1 g, Fat: 2.6 g, % Cal. from fat: 11*

Bouillabaisse

❌ 〜 ❄

This simple bouillabaisse is lovely for company. I often complete the first four steps ahead and add the fish when we sit down to our first course. It cooks while we eat our appetizer.

1 28-ounce can tomatoes, chopped (including liquid)
1 cup chopped onion
½ cup chopped celery
1 teaspoon chicken bouillon powder
½ teaspoon thyme
½ teaspoon basil
¼ teaspoon red pepper flakes
Dash Tabasco sauce
1 bay leaf
1 pound firm fish (I use snapper), cut in pieces
½ pound shrimp, peeled and deveined, or scallops

1. Combine 2 tablespoons tomato liquid with onion and celery in a 3-quart casserole. Cover and cook in microwave on High for 3 to 4 minutes.

2. Add tomatoes to casserole with bouillon powder and spices.

3. Cover and cook in microwave on High for 18 minutes. Add fish and shrimp. Stir well. Cover and cook on High for 4 minutes. Let stand for 5 minutes. Discard bay leaf.

Makes 4 servings. PER SERVING: *Calories: 223, Protein: 35.3 g, Carbohydrates: 14.4 g, Fat: 2.5 g, % Cal. from fat: 10*

Shrimp and Peppers

🕐 🍴

Even though shrimp is higher in cholesterol than poultry, beef or other fish, it can still be part of a low-cholesterol diet. Shrimp has a very low fat content and is rich in omega-3 fatty acids, which help lower cholesterol.

4 cloves garlic, minced
1 green onion, chopped
3 tablespoons chopped fresh parsley
3 tablespoons lemon juice
1 tablespoon basil
½ teaspoon pepper
⅛ teaspoon cayenne pepper
1½ pounds shrimp, peeled and deveined
1 red pepper, sliced
2 teaspoons oil

1. Combine garlic, onion, parsley, lemon juice, basil, pepper and cayenne. Stir in shrimp and marinate 15 minutes.

2. In wok or large non-stick skillet, sauté red pepper in oil until tender-crisp.

3. Add shrimp and marinade and cook for 2 to 3 minutes, or until shrimp is opaque.

Makes 4 servings. PER SERVING: *Calories: 214, Protein: 35 g, Carbohydrates: 5.0 g, Fat: 5.2 g, % Cal. from fat: 23*

Sesame Tiger Shrimp

☉ ✂

When you feel like splurging, this dish is absolutely fantastic. Tiger shrimp are more expensive than smaller shrimp, but the larger shells lead to less waste per pound.

1 teaspoon sesame oil
1 tablespoon finely chopped fresh ginger
2 tablespoons soy sauce
1½ pounds tiger shrimp, peeled and deveined
2 teaspoons sesame seeds
2 green onions, sliced

1. Heat a large non-stick skillet or wok over medium heat. Add sesame oil and ginger; cook for 1 minute.

2. Add soy sauce, shrimp and sesame seeds. Cook for 2 to 3 minutes, tossing to coat shrimp with sesame seeds.

3. Add green onion and cook 1 minute, or until shrimp is opaque.

Makes 4 servings. PER SERVING: *Calories: 207, Protein: 35.6 g, Carbohydrates: 3.0 g, Fat: 4.8 g, % Cal. from fat: 22*

"Outstanding" Shrimp

✗

The most frequent comment I receive when serving this dish is that it's outstanding.

1 tablespoon lime juice
¼ teaspoon salt
½ teaspoon pepper
¾ teaspoon paprika
1½ pounds shrimp, peeled and deveined
1 tablespoon oil
1 medium onion, chopped
3 cloves garlic, minced
½ cup chopped fresh parsley
1 teaspoon curry powder
¼ teaspoon thyme
⅛ to ¼ teaspoon red pepper flakes
½ cup chicken broth

1. Combine lime juice with salt, pepper and paprika. Toss mixture with shrimp.

2. Heat large non-stick skillet or wok over medium heat. Add oil, onion, garlic, parsley, curry, thyme and red pepper flakes. Sauté 1 minute.

3. Add shrimp and chicken broth. Cook 3 minutes. Remove shrimp with slotted spoon and set aside. Boil sauce until reduced by half.

4. Return shrimp to sauce and heat through.

Makes 4 servings. PER SERVING: *Calories: 230, Protein: 35.7 g, Carbohydrates: 5.0 g, Fat: 6.6 g, % Cal. from fat: 27*

Ceviche

🕐 ✂

On a hot summer evening, my husband and I enjoy this dish with some grainy bread and a salad. The lime juice causes the scallops to become firm and taste cooked.

1   pound scallops
⅓   cup fresh lime juice
½   large green pepper, diced
½   large red pepper, diced
½   cup diced red onion
¼   cup chopped fresh parsley
¼   teaspoon salt
⅛   teaspoon pepper
⅛   teaspoon red pepper flakes

1. Combine scallops and lime juice. Refrigerate at least 4 hours.

2. Drain scallops. Add remaining ingredients to scallops and mix well. Chill at least 30 minutes.

Makes 2 main-course or 4 appetizer servings. PER APPETIZER SERVING: *Calories: 119, Protein: 19.6 g, Carbohydrates: 7.5 g, Fat: 0.95 g, % Cal. from fat: 7*

Company Chicken

◷ ✕

I have called this recipe Company Chicken because it can be prepared ahead, allowing you time with your guests.

⅔ cup thinly sliced onion
4 skinless, boneless chicken breasts (about 1 pound total)
1 green pepper, sliced
1½ cups sliced mushrooms
10 cherry tomatoes, halved
½ cup chopped fresh parsley
½ cup dry white wine
2 tablespoons lemon juice
⅛ teaspoon pepper

1. Arrange onion slices in baking dish sprayed with cooking spray. Place chicken breasts on top.

2. Toss together green pepper, mushrooms, cherry tomatoes and parsley; spread over chicken breasts.

3. Combine wine, lemon juice and pepper. Pour over all.

4. Cover and bake at 375°F for 35 to 40 minutes.

Makes 4 servings. PER SERVING: *Calories: 195, Protein: 28.3 g, Carbohydrates: 7.9 g, Fat: 3.4 g, % Cal. from fat: 16*

Sweet and Sour Chicken

◷ ❄

This recipe is particularly easy to prepare if you use TGTBT Sweet and Sour Sauce. If it's not available, use my recipe on page 171.

4 skinless, boneless chicken breasts (about 1 pound total)
½ cup Sweet and Sour Sauce

1. Brush chicken breasts with sauce.

2. Broil or barbecue breasts 6 to 7 minutes per side, brushing with extra sauce during cooking.

Makes 4 servings. PER SERVING: *Calories: 153, Protein: 27.5 g, Carbohydrates: 2.0 g, Fat: 3.0 g, % Cal. from fat: 19 ·*

Chicken Mediterranean

✄ $

This chicken dish is simple to prepare, but does take some time to bake. If you want to get a head start, prepare it up to step 4 and refrigerate.

4 skinless, boneless chicken breasts (about 1 pound total)
½ teaspoon salt
¼ teaspoon pepper
1 19-ounce can tomatoes, chopped (including liquid)
1 cup sliced zucchini
1 cup sliced mushrooms
⅓ cup chopped onion
1 clove garlic, minced
2 teaspoons basil
1 bay leaf

1. Season chicken with salt and pepper. Place in baking dish and bake at 425°F for 20 minutes.

2 Remove chicken from oven and pour off any fat.

3. In a bowl combine remaining ingredients. Pour over chicken.

4. Cover and bake at 350°F for 45 minutes. Remove bay leaf.

Makes 4 servings. PER SERVING: *Calories: 185, Protein: 28.9 g, Carbohydrates: 9.0 g, Fat: 3.5 g, % Cal. from fat: 17*

Microwave Chicken Dijon

🕐 🍴 ≋ ❄

This recipe is special enough for company and a cinch to prepare. You can vary the taste slightly by using another variety of mustard.

2 cloves garlic
2 green onions, sliced
¼ cup Dijon mustard
2 tablespoons white wine
1 tablespoon fresh lemon juice
¼ teaspoon tarragon
Freshly ground pepper to taste
4 skinless, boneless chicken breasts (about 1 pound total)

1. In a 10-inch glass pie plate, combine garlic and green onions with 2 tablespoons water. Cover and cook in microwave on High for 1 minute.

2. Stir in mustard, wine, lemon juice, tarragon and pepper.

3. Roll chicken breasts in mixture and place around outer rim of dish. Cover with waxed paper and cook in microwave on High for 3 minutes.

4. Turn chicken over and spoon sauce over breasts. Cover again and cook in microwave on High for 3 to 5 minutes, or until chicken is cooked through.

Makes 4 servings. PER SERVING: *Calories: 163, Protein: 27.6 g, Carbohydrates: 2.0 g, Fat: 3.7 g, % Cal. from fat: 22*

20 Clove Garlic Chicken

The best thing about this recipe is the amazing aroma that will permeate your home. Don't be frightened by the number of garlic cloves; the longer they bake, the sweeter they become.

4 stalks celery, cut in ¼-inch slices
1 large onion, sliced
2 tablespoons chopped fresh parsley (or 2 teaspoons dried)
1 teaspoon tarragon
4 skinless, boneless chicken breasts (about 1 pound total)
½ cup dry white wine
½ teaspoon salt
¼ teaspoon pepper
20 cloves garlic, peeled

1. Combine celery, onion, parsley and tarragon in a casserole dish.

2. Lay chicken breasts over the vegetable mixture. Pour wine over chicken. Sprinkle with salt and pepper. Distribute the garlic cloves throughout the casserole.

3. Cover the casserole tightly with foil, and bake at 325°F for 1 hour, or until chicken is opaque and cooked through.

Makes 4 servings. PER SERVING: *Calories: 201, Protein: 28.3 g, Carbohydrates: 9.1 g, Fat: 3.2 g, % Cal. from fat: 15*

Tropical Chicken

⊘ ✗

I discovered this great combination of sweet fruit and chicken quite by accident when I planned to make another chicken dish and found I didn't have enough pineapple. I mixed what I had with some banana and was delighted with the result.

1 small ripe banana, sliced
½ cup pineapple chunks packed in their own juice
3 tablespoons lemon juice
3 tablespoons soy sauce
¼ cup chopped fresh parsley
4 skinless, boneless chicken breasts (about 1 pound total)

1. Place banana and pineapple in a non-stick skillet sprayed with cooking spray. Sauté fruit for 3 minutes, then stir in the lemon juice, soy sauce and parsley.

2. Place chicken breasts in a baking dish. Pour fruit mixture over and bake at 350°F for 1 hour.

Makes 4 servings. PER SERVING: *Calories: 198, Protein: 28.4 g, Carbohydrates: 13.6 g, Fat: 3.2 g, % Cal. from fat: 15*

Yogurt-Baked Chicken

◷ ✖

This easy recipe is sure to be a hit even with those who dislike yogurt. The mixture of soy sauce and Parmesan cheese gives it a wonderful flavour and keeps the chicken breasts moist and juicy.

4   skinless, boneless chicken breasts (about 1 pound total)
1   cup plain low-fat yogurt
2   cloves garlic, minced
1   tablespoon soy sauce
1   teaspoon paprika
1   teaspoon oregano
3   tablespoons grated Parmesan cheese

1. Place chicken breasts in a baking dish sprayed with cooking spray.

2. In small bowl, combine ½ cup yogurt, garlic, soy sauce, paprika and oregano. Spread over chicken.

3. Bake, uncovered, at 400°F for 30 minutes.

4. Stir Parmesan cheese into remaining yogurt. Spread over chicken.

5. Bake 10 minutes, or until bubbling.

Makes 4 servings. PER SERVING: *Calories: 200, Protein: 31.7 g, Carbohydrates: 5.0 g, Fat: 5.0 g, % Cal. from fat: 24*

Mexican Chicken Chili

🕐 💲 ❄️

This chicken chili is great served over brown rice or pasta. To keep the calories low, substitute a bed of steamed cabbage for the rice or pasta.

½ pound skinless, boneless chicken, cut in strips
⅓ cup chopped onion
⅓ cup chopped green pepper
1 clove garlic, minced
1 14-ounce can kidney beans, undrained
1 14-ounce can tomatoes, chopped (including liquid)
½ teaspoon cumin
¼ teaspoon salt
⅛ teaspoon pepper
⅛ teaspoon cayenne
⅛ teaspoon oregano

1. Spray a large skillet with cooking spray and place over medium heat until hot. Add chicken and cook 1 minute.

2. Add onion, green pepper and garlic. Cook another 2 minutes.

3. Stir in remaining ingredients and cook over low heat for 20 minutes.

Makes 4 servings. PER SERVING: *Calories: 214, Protein: 24.7 g, Carbohydrates: 23.2 g, Fat: 2.6 g, % Cal. from fat: 11*

Chicken à l'Orange

✂ ❄

You'll love the combination of orange and ginger in this recipe. The orange slices make the dish look as good as it tastes.

4   skinless, boneless chicken breasts (about 1 pound total)
¼   teaspoon paprika
⅛   teaspoon salt
⅛   teaspoon pepper
1   orange
2   tablespoons lemon juice
1   cup water
2   teaspoons Splenda sweetener
1   teaspoon curry powder
2   cloves garlic, minced
1   tablespoon minced fresh ginger

1. Arrange chicken breasts in a baking dish. Sprinkle with paprika, salt and pepper.

2. Grate the orange rind. In a small bowl, combine lemon juice, water and sweetener. Stir until dissolved. Add orange peel, curry, garlic and ginger. Mix well.

3. Pour mixture over chicken. Cover with foil and bake at 400°F for 20 minutes.

4. Turn chicken and baste well. Cover and bake for another 20 minutes.

5. Remove foil and baste. Slice orange and arrange slices over chicken. Bake another 5 minutes to heat oranges.

Makes 4 servings. PER SERVING: *Calories: 162, Protein: 27.2 g, Carbohydrates: 4.9 g, Fat: 3.1 g, % Cal. from fat: 18*

Chicken Loaf

🕐 $ ❄

This chicken loaf is a tasty alternative to meat loaf. Serve it cold the next day with a salad, or in a sandwich. Use mustard as the spread, instead of butter or mayo.

1 egg
2 egg whites
½ cup plain low-fat yogurt
2 tablespoons Dijon mustard
¼ teaspoon salt
¼ teaspoon pepper
1 stalk celery, chopped
1 onion, chopped
1 clove garlic, minced
2 pounds ground chicken
1 cup dry bread crumbs

1. Combine all ingredients, except chicken and bread crumbs, in large bowl.

2. Add 1 pound chicken and ½ cup bread crumbs. Mix with your hands or a large fork. Add remaining chicken and crumbs and mix until blended.

3. Put mixture into a large loaf pan or casserole dish sprayed with cooking spray.

4. Cover loosely with foil and bake at 350°F for 1 hour. Uncover and cook an additional 15 to 20 minutes, or until golden brown.

Makes 8 servings. PER SERVING: *Calories: 214, Protein: 28.6 g, Carbohydrates: 11.8 g, Fat: 5.1 g, % Cal. from fat: 22*

Sweet and Spicy Turkey Loaf

🕐 $ ❄

I rarely use garlic powder since fresh is so much better, but in this recipe it tastes just fine. Ground turkey has become a popular alternative to ground beef and chicken.

1 pound ground turkey
¼ teaspoon pepper
¼ teaspoon ground nutmeg
¼ teaspoon garlic powder
1 tablespoon sweet relish
3 tablespoons ketchup
1 teaspoon prepared mustard
½ cup finely chopped onions

1. In large bowl, combine all ingredients. Mix well.

2. Put mixture into a medium-sized loaf pan.

3. Bake, uncovered, at 350°F for 1 hour.

Makes 4 servings. PER SERVING: *Calories: 186, Protein: 20.3 g, Carbohydrates: 6.1 g, Fat: 8.6 g, % Cal. from fat: 42*

Turkey Burgers

🕐 $ ❄

If you have a stove-top grill, it's ideal for this recipe. The steam created by the boiling water keeps the burgers moist. For a lower-fat burger, ask your butcher to grind turkey breast meat without skin.

1 pound ground turkey
2 teaspoons Dijon mustard
Salt and pepper to taste

1. Combine all ingredients and form into four patties.

2. If using a stove-top grill, fill reservoir with $1\frac{1}{2}$ cups water. Heat grill on high for 6 to 8 minutes.

3. Cook burgers on grill, or broil or barbecue, approximately 5 minutes per side.

Makes 4 servings. PER SERVING: *Calories: 163, Protein: 20 g, Carbohydrates: 0.17 g, Fat: 8.6 g, % Cal. from fat: 49*

Baked Turkey Breast with BBQ Sauce

Turkey is a low-fat source of protein. But commercial barbecue sauce is high in sugar. If you dilute it with soy sauce and Dijon, you can use less. The TGTBT Lite Gourmet BBQ Sauce has only 12 calories per tablespoon, compared to 30 calories per tablespoon for the regular varieties.

1 skinless turkey breast (about 2 pounds)
¼ cup barbecue sauce
1½ tablespoons soy sauce
1 tablespoon Dijon mustard

1. Place turkey breast in baking pan.

2. Combine barbecue sauce, soy sauce and mustard. Brush on turkey.

3. Bake, uncovered, at 375°F for 15 minutes. Reduce temperature to 325°F and continue baking for 1 hour, or until turkey is cooked.

Makes 6 servings of approximately 4 ounces each. PER SERVING: *Calories: 180, Protein: 37.7 g, Carbohydrates: 1.8 g, Fat: 1.2 g, % Cal. from fat: 7*

Beef Kabobs

Almost any vegetables can be used in these kabobs. One of my favourites is Brussels sprouts. If you use them, microwave them for a few minutes first to soften, since they take longer to cook than other vegetables.

- 1 pound lean beef, cut into 1-inch cubes
- 1 medium onion, peeled, quartered lengthwise and separated into pieces
- 1 medium zucchini, cut into ¼-inch slices
- 1 red pepper, cut into 1-inch squares
- 1 green pepper, cut into 1-inch squares
- 8 cherry tomatoes
- ¼ cup Sweet and Sour Sauce (see page 171)

1. Arrange meat and vegetables alternately on metal skewers.

2. Brush with Sweet and Sour Sauce.

3. Broil or barbecue for 8 to 10 minutes, or until desired doneness, turning several times and brushing kabobs with remaining sauce.

Makes 4 servings. PER SERVING: *Calories: 212, Protein: 25.7 g, Carbohydrates: 8.2 g, Fat: 8.3 g, % Cal. from fat: 36*

Szechwan Beef

If you like really spicy food, increase the amount of red pepper flakes in this recipe.

2 teaspoons oil
2 green onions, sliced
2 cloves garlic, minced
¼ teaspoon red pepper flakes
1 pound flank or round steak, thinly sliced
1 tablespoon cornstarch
1 tablespoon soy sauce
½ teaspoon sugar
½ cup chicken broth

1. Heat oil in large non-stick skillet or wok over medium-high heat. Add onions, garlic and red pepper flakes. Stir-fry for 10 seconds.

2. Add steak and stir-fry for a few minutes, or until meat is browned.

3. Combine remaining ingredients in small bowl. Add to skillet and stir-fry until sauce thickens.

Makes 4 servings. PER SERVING: *Calories: 199, Protein: 26.6 g, Carbohydrates: 3.6 g, Fat: 7.9 g, % Cal. from fat: 37*

Sukiyaki

This sukiyaki can also be made with chicken or pork strips. If you don't own a wok, use a large non-stick skillet.

1	pound flank or round steak, thinly sliced
1	teaspoon oil
3	cups bean sprouts
1	cup sliced mushrooms
1	large onion, sliced
1	green pepper, sliced
1	10-ounce can water chestnuts, drained and sliced
½	cup beef broth
3	tablespoons soy sauce
1	tablespoon cornstarch

1. Spray wok with cooking spray and heat over medium-high heat. Add sliced beef and stir-fry for 2 to 3 minutes, or until meat is brown. Remove from pan.

2. Add oil, bean sprouts, mushrooms, onion, green pepper and water chestnuts. Stir-fry for 2 minutes.

3. Combine remaining ingredients in small bowl. Mix well and add to wok. Stir-fry mixture a few minutes to thicken sauce.

4. Add meat and stir-fry to heat through.

Makes 4 servings. PER SERVING: *Calories: 251, Protein: 30.5 g, Carbohydrates: 17.3 g, Fat: 6.9 g, % Cal. from fat: 25*

Teriyaki Steak

In many recipes, a good substitute for honey and sugar is frozen pineapple juice concentrate. Slice off the amount you need and put the rest back in the freezer.

2 tablespoons soy sauce
4 ounces frozen pineapple juice concentrate
2 cloves garlic, minced
1 tablespoon minced fresh ginger
1 pound flank or round steak

1. Combine soy sauce, juice concentrate, garlic and ginger.

2. Marinate steak in sauce for at least 2 hours. (Overnight is better.)

3. Broil or barbecue for 4 to 5 minutes per side, or until desired doneness. Slice into 4 portions.

Makes 4 servings. PER SERVING: *Calories: 231, Protein: 26.8 g, Carbohydrates: 17.4 g, Fat: 5.5 g, % Cal. from fat: 22*

Roasted Leg of Lamb

Inserting garlic slivers into lamb before cooking it produces a roast with a wonderful flavour. The leftover lamb makes a super souvlaki sandwich when stuffed into a pita with tzatziki.

1 3-pound leg of lamb
3 cloves garlic, peeled and slivered
Salt and pepper to taste

1. Make small slits in lamb with tip of a sharp knife. Insert garlic slivers.

2. Place meat on a rack in a roasting pan. Sprinkle with salt and pepper.

3. Roast, uncovered, at 325°F for 1¾ hours, or until meat thermometer registers 175°F.

Makes 6 to 8 servings. PER 3 OUNCE SERVING: *Calories: 201, Protein: 35.5 g, Carbohydrates: 0.37 g, Fat: 6.4, % Cal. from fat: 29*

Baked Pork Chops

◷

The cornstarch causes the orange juice mixture to thicken and become a glaze as the pork chops bake.

- 4 pork chops (about 1 pound total)
- ½ cup unsweetened orange juice
- 1 tablespoon soy sauce
- 2 teaspoons cornstarch
- 1 teaspoon honey
- ¼ teaspoon dry mustard

1. Place pork chops in baking dish sprayed with cooking spray.

2. Combine remaining ingredients. Mix well and pour over pork chops.

3. Bake, covered, at 350°F covered for 1 hour.

Makes 4 servings. PER SERVING: *Calories: 176, Protein: 26 g, Carbohydrates: 6.1 g, Fat: 4.5 g, % Cal. from fat: 24*

Stir-Fry Pork and Cellophane Noodles

✂

Various types of noodles work well in this recipe. If cellophane noodles are unavailable, use rice vermicelli, bean thread or angel hair pasta.

Marinade:
- 2 cloves garlic, minced
- 1 green onion, sliced
- 3 tablespoons rice vinegar
- 1 tablespoon soy sauce
- 1 tablespoon sesame seeds
- ½ teaspoon sugar

PHOTO: *Fruit Tart (page 244)*

1 pound pork tenderloin, cut into strips
3 ounces cellophane noodles
1 tablespoon sesame oil
2 small carrots, sliced
1 medium onion, sliced
¾ cup sliced mushrooms
1 red pepper, sliced
1 zucchini, sliced
⅛ teaspoon red pepper flakes

1. Combine marinade ingredients. Pour over pork and marinate for 1 hour.

2. Cover noodles with warm water and soak for 30 minutes. Drain and rinse.

3. Heat 1 teaspoon oil in a large non-stick skillet or wok over high heat. Add pork and stir-fry for 4 to 5 minutes. Remove pork from pan and set aside.

4. Add 1 teaspoon oil to skillet. Add carrots and onion. Stir-fry for 2 to 3 minutes. Add mushrooms, red pepper and zucchini. Stir-fry until peppers are tender but still crisp. Remove vegetables from pan. Set aside.

5. Add last teaspoon of oil and stir-fry the noodles for 1 minute. Place noodles in warmed serving dish.

6. Return pork and vegetables to pan. Stir in red pepper flakes. Cook 2 to 3 minutes to heat through and blend flavours.

7. Serve pork mixture on top of noodles.

Makes 4 servings. PER SERVING: *Calories: 292, Protein: 26.3 g, Carbohydrates: 29.5 g, Fat: 7.6 g, % Cal. from fat: 23*

PHOTO: *Roasted Leeks with Parmesan (page 228);
Sweet Potato Oven Fries (page 237)*

Pork Chops with Dijon Mustard

The combination of soy sauce and Dijon mustard gives this marinade a nice tang. I keep a bottle of cheap wine on hand for cooking. It adds as much flavour as the more expensive ones.

¼ cup dry white wine
3 tablespoons soy sauce
1½ tablespoons Dijon mustard
1 clove garlic, minced
4 pork chops (about 1 pound total)

1. Combine wine, soy sauce, mustard and garlic. Pour over pork chops. Marinate several hours or overnight.

2. Broil or barbecue, basting with marinade, for 5 minutes per side, or until desired doneness.

Makes 4 servings. PER SERVING: *Calories: 173, Protein: 26.9 g, Carbohydrates: 1.8 g, Fat: 4.7 g, % Cal. from fat: 25*

Veal Loaf

The advantage of baking a loaf on a rack is that the fat drips into the pan instead of cooking into the meat.

1 pound lean ground veal
1 egg white
1 clove garlic, minced
½ teaspoon rosemary, crumbled
Pepper to taste

1. Combine all ingredients and shape into a loaf.

2. Place on a rack in a shallow baking pan with a little water in it (to prevent a fat fire).

3. Bake, uncovered, at 350°F for 1 hour.

Makes 4 servings. PER SERVING: *Calories: 169, Protein: 22.8 g, Carbohydrates: 0.33 g, Fat: 7.6 g, % Cal. from fat: 43*

Veal al Limone

When veal al limone is served in restaurants, a rich butter sauce accompanies it. This sauce tastes equally good — without any added fat.

1 pound veal scallopini
½ teaspoon grated lemon peel
2 tablespoons lemon juice
1 tablespoon water
1 teaspoon honey
1 teaspoon Worcestershire sauce
½ teaspoon Dijon mustard
⅛ teaspoon pepper

1. Cut veal into four pieces.

2. Combine remaining ingredients and pour over veal. Marinate several hours or overnight.

3. Broil, basting with marinade, for 3 minutes per side, or until desired doneness.

Makes 4 servings. PER SERVING: *Calories: 136, Protein: 23.1 g, Carbohydrates: 2.2 g, Fat: 3.2 g, % Cal. from fat: 23*

Roasted Leeks with Parmesan

✴ $

The addition of Parmesan cheese makes this a special dish. I also enjoy leeks without the Parmesan, but cooked a little longer until the ends become quite brown and crisp.

3 large leeks
Pepper to taste
3 tablespoons grated Parmesan cheese

1. Split leeks in half lengthwise and wash thoroughly. Cut leeks in half crosswise and place on dinner plate with 3 tablespoons water. Cover and cook in microwave on High for 5 minutes to soften.

2. Place leeks on cookie sheet sprayed with cooking spray. Spray leeks as well. Sprinkle with pepper.

3. Bake at 400°F for 15 minutes. Sprinkle with Parmesan cheese and bake an additional 8 minutes.

Makes 4 servings. PER SERVING: *Calories: 74, Protein: 2.9 g, Carbohydrates: 13.3 g, Fat: 1.4 g, % Cal. from fat: 16*

Spaghetti Squash

$

Spaghetti squash looks like pasta when pulled out of its skin — it separates into strands. It is similar in calories to zucchini, rather than starchier winter squash, such as acorn or butternut.

1 large spaghetti squash
2 cups tomato sauce
4 ounces low-fat mozzarella, shredded

1. Cut squash in half lengthwise and remove seeds. Place squash cut side down on cookie sheet sprayed with cooking spray. Bake at 350°F for 1 hour, or until squash is tender.

2. Bring tomato sauce to a boil. Reduce heat, then stir in cheese.

3. Remove squash from shell with a fork. Add strands to tomato sauce and mix well.

Makes 4 servings. PER SERVING: *Calories: 145, Protein: 9.5 g, Carbohydrates: 17.1 g, Fat: 5.1 g, % Cal. from fat: 31*

Skillet Squash
✂ $

Here's another recipe that is great for company and can be prepared ahead of time — if you cook it for only 10 minutes, then simmer an additional 5 minutes before serving.

1 large onion, sliced
4 medium zucchini (preferably 2 green and 2 yellow), sliced
1 large tomato, cut into chunks
2 tablespoons balsamic vinegar
1 tablespoon oregano
1 teaspoon basil
Salt and pepper to taste

1. Place onion in large non-stick skillet with 3 tablespoons of water and cook over medium heat until softened.

2. Add remaining ingredients, cover, stirring occasionally and simmer 15 minutes, or until vegetables are tender.

Makes 4 servings. PER SERVING: *Calories: 47, Protein: 2.8 g, Carbohydrates: 10.3 g, Fat: 0.45 g, % Cal. from fat: 7*

Sweet and Sour Baked Squash

⊘ $

Use TGTBT Sweet and Sour Sauce and this recipe can be prepared in minutes. Or use my recipe for Sweet and Sour Sauce on page 171.

2 pepper squash
⅓ cup Sweet and Sour Sauce

1. Cut squash in half and scoop out seeds. Place squash cut side up on baking sheet. Brush cut edges and inside of squash with sauce, and pour any remaining sauce in cavity.

2. Bake at 350°F for 45 minutes, or until tender.

Makes 4 servings. PER SERVING: *Calories: 93, Protein: 2.2 g, Carbohydrates: 23.8 g, Fat: 0.21 g, % Cal. from fat: 2*

Grilled Eggplant

⊘ $

Most eggplant recipes use a generous amount of oil, which the eggplant soaks up. I find that by spraying the eggplant with cooking spray, no oil is required.

1 large eggplant, unpeeled (about 2 pounds)
Salt and pepper to taste

1. Cut eggplant into ½-inch slices.

2. Lay slices on cookie sheet sprayed with cooking spray. Spray eggplant. Season with salt and pepper.

3. Broil 10 minutes on each side.

Makes 4 servings. PER SERVING: *Calories: 65, Protein: 2.4 g, Carbohydrates: 14.2 g, Fat: 0.97, % Cal. from fat: 12*

Szechwan Eggplant

✻ $

This dish goes well with grilled meat, fish and chicken. My husband and I especially enjoy it along with Oven-Cooked Barbecue Tofu. To make this recipe spicier, more cayenne or red pepper flakes can be used.

1 large eggplant, unpeeled(about 2 pounds)
1 teaspoon sesame oil
1 large clove garlic, minced
1 tablespoon minced fresh ginger
1 tablespoon vinegar
1 tablespoon soy sauce
2 teaspoons Splenda sweetener
1 cup water
1 tablespoon cornstarch
Dash cayenne pepper

1. Slice eggplant into 2-inch finger-like strips.

2. Spray wok with cooking spray and heat over medium heat. Add eggplant and stir-fry for 15 to 20 minutes, or until soft.

3. Remove eggplant. Add oil, garlic and ginger. Cook for 1 minute.

4. Combine remaining ingredients in small bowl. Mix well and add to wok. Bring to a boil. Add eggplant.

5. Cook and stir 3 minutes, or until sauce is thick.

Makes 4 servings. PER SERVING: *Calories: 82, Protein: 2.9 g, Carbohydrates: 17.1 g, Fat: 1.3 g, % Cal. from fat: 13*

Barbecued Vegetable Packages

✗

I love serving my guests their own individual packages of vegetables. They always comment on the wonderful aroma and colourful mixture when they open up the foil. The percent of calories from fat in this dish may appear to be high, but each low-cal serving only contains 1 teaspoon of oil (fat).

2 large tomatoes, cut into chunks
1 medium eggplant, unpeeled, cut into chunks
1 red or green pepper, sliced
1 medium zucchini, sliced
1 medium onion, sliced
Garlic powder and oregano to taste
Salt and pepper to taste
4 teaspoons olive oil

1. Cut four pieces of aluminum foil about 12 inches square. Divide vegetables evenly, positioning in centre of each foil square.

2. Sprinkle with herbs and spices. Drizzle 1 teaspoon oil on each portion. Close vegetable packages, folding edges to seal.

3. Barbecue for 30 minutes, turning occasionally.

Makes 4 servings. PER SERVING: *Calories: 85, Protein: 1.9 g, Carbohydrates: 10.1 g, Fat: 5.0 g, % Cal. from fat: 48*

Grilled Vegetable Ratatouille

❄

In this recipe, the extra step of grilling the vegetables replaces the traditional method of frying both the eggplant and the zucchini. If you want to simplify the recipe, combine all the ingredients and cook over medium heat for 1½ hours, or until tender. However, I feel the flavour that develops from cooking the vegetables first is well worth the effort. For a hearty dinner, serve this dish over rice. It's also great on its own, with some Parmesan cheese sprinkled on top.

1 large eggplant (about 2½ pounds), unpeeled, cubed
4 large zucchini, cut in ½-inch slices
1 red pepper
1 green pepper
3 medium onions, sliced
4 cloves garlic, minced
1 28-ounce can tomatoes, chopped (including liquid)
1 tablespoon oregano
1 teaspoon basil
¼ teaspoon salt
⅛ teaspoon pepper
1 bay leaf
1 cup chopped fresh parsley

1. Spray three cookie sheets with cooking spray. Place eggplant and zucchini on sheets and spray vegetables lightly.

2. Bake, using both oven racks, at 425°F for 15 minutes. Remove lower cookie sheet and broil two top cookie sheets for 8 to 10 minutes. Remove these from oven and broil third sheet 8 to 10 minutes.

3. Place both peppers on one stove element turned to high. When peppers start to blacken, turn them and continue to blacken all sides. When cool enough to handle, cut into cubes and remove seeds. If you have a gas stove, cube the peppers and bake at 425°F for 15 minutes on a cookie sheet sprayed with cooking spray.

4. Place onions and garlic in bowl with 3 tablespoons water. Cook, covered, in microwave on High for 5 minutes.

5. Place eggplant, zucchini, peppers, onions and garlic in large pot. Add tomatoes and seasonings. Simmer, uncovered, for 30 minutes, stirring occasionally.

6. Add parsley and simmer 15 minutes. Remove bay leaf.

Makes 12 cups. PER 1 CUP SERVING: *Calories: 63, Protein: 3.0 g, Carbohydrates: 14.2 g, Fat: 0.43 g, % Cal. from fat: 5*

Grilled Zucchini

🕐 $

An easy way of cooking zucchini is to turn your stove element to high heat and lay the strips of zucchini across it. If you cook with a gas stove, a more conventional method follows.

3 large zucchini
Oregano and pepper to taste

1. Slice zucchini lengthwise into ¼- to ½-inch strips.

2. Lay zucchini on cookie sheets sprayed with cooking spray. Spray zucchini as well and sprinkle with seasonings.

3. Brown under broiler 5 to 6 minutes per side.

Makes 4 servings. PER SERVING: *Calories: 20, Protein: 1.6 g, Carbohydrates: 4.1 g, Fat: 0.20 g, % Cal. from fat: 7*

Chinese Green Beans

🍴 $

Increase the amount of cayenne pepper in this dish if you enjoy very spicy Szechwan food. These beans make a terrific accompaniment to grilled meat and chicken.

1 pound green beans, cut in 1½-inch pieces
1 green onion, sliced
1 clove garlic, minced
3 tablespoons rice vinegar
1 tablespoon minced fresh ginger
1 tablespoon soy sauce
1 teaspoon honey
1 teaspoon sesame oil
⅛ teaspoon cayenne pepper

1. Place green beans in a bowl with 3 tablespoons water. Cook, covered, in microwave on High for 6 minutes. (Or steam on stove-top for 6 to 8 minutes, or until tender-crisp.)

2. Combine remaining ingredients in small bowl.

3. In large non-stick skillet, heat soy mixture until just boiling. Add cooked green beans and toss to coat. Cook 1 minute to heat through.

Makes 4 servings. PER SERVING: *Calories: 57, Protein: 2.5 g, Carbohydrates: 11 g, Fat: 1.2 g, % Cal. from fat: 18*

Oriental Cabbage

$

Cabbage is a member of the Brassica family of vegetables. Other members include Brussels sprouts, broccoli and cauliflower. All the Brassica vegetables contain indoles, which have been shown to have anti-carcinogenic properties.

1 large onion, sliced
1 clove garlic, minced
1 teaspoon minced fresh ginger
2 teaspoons sesame oil
6 cups sliced cabbage, ¼-inch thick
2 tablespoons soy sauce

1. Place onion in bowl with 2 tablespoons water. Cover and cook in microwave on High for 3 minutes.

2. Put onion in large non-stick skillet with remaining ingredients and 1 tablespoon water.

3. Cook, covered, over medium-low heat, stirring occasionally, until cabbage is tender, about 20 minutes.

Makes 4 to 6 servings. PER SERVING: *Calories: 43, Protein: 1.6 g, Carbohydrates: 6.2 g, Fat: 1.6 g, % Cal. from fat: 32*

Brussels Sprouts with Mustard Sauce

⊙ $

In addition to belonging to the Brassica family of vegetables, which display anti-cancer properties, Brussels sprouts are a good source of vitamins A and C, potassium and iron.

1   pound Brussels sprouts, trimmed
1   cup beef broth
1   tablespoon Dijon mustard
2   teaspoons lemon juice
1   teaspoon thyme

1. Place Brussels sprouts in a bowl with 3 tablespoons water. Cover and cook in microwave on High for 10 minutes, or until tender. (Or steam on stovetop for 10 minutes.) Cover to keep warm.

2. Combine remaining ingredients in large skillet and cook approximately 3 minutes, or until mixture reduces.

3. Add cooked Brussels sprouts and toss to coat.

Makes 4 servings. PER SERVING: *Calories: 57, Protein: 4.7 g, Carbohydrates: 10.6 g, Fat: 0.65 g, % Cal. from fat: 9*

Oven Fries

⊙ $

In most traditional recipes for oven fries the potatoes are brushed with oil, adding unnecessary fat to an ideal substitute for french fries.

3 medium baking potatoes, unpeeled (about 1 pound total)
Salt and pepper to taste

1. Cut potatoes into ¼-inch slices. Place on cookie sheets sprayed with cooking spray. Sprinkle with salt and pepper.

2. Bake at 425°F for 20 to 25 minutes, turning after 15 minutes.

Makes 4 servings. PER SERVING: *Calories: 124, Protein: 2.6 g, Carbohydrates: 28.6 g, Fat: 0.11 g, % Cal. from fat: 1*

Sweet Potato Oven Fries

⊘ $

Try this recipe for a change from traditional baking potatoes. These are so delicious you won't even need to season them.

3 medium sweet potatoes, unpeeled (about 1 pound total)

1. Cut potatoes into ¼-inch slices. Place on cookie sheets sprayed with cooking spray.

2. Bake at 425°F for 20 to 25 minutes, turning after 15 minutes.

Makes 4 servings. PER SERVING: *Calories: 140, Protein: 2.6 g, Carbohydrates: 32 g, Fat: 0.11 g, % Cal. from fat: 1*

Barbecued Potatoes and Onions

⊘ $

To keep your kitchen cool on a hot summer night, cook these potatoes on the barbecue along with some fish or chicken.

3 medium potatoes, unpeeled, cubed
2 medium onions, sliced
1 tablespoon oil
Salt, pepper and paprika to taste

1. Cut a large sheet of heavy-duty aluminium foil (or fold regular strength foil to double thickness) and place potatoes and onions in centre.

2. Drizzle oil over potatoes and sprinkle with seasonings. Wrap foil, sealing ends well.

3. Place on barbecue grill about 4 inches from coals. Cook for 30 minutes, turning package after 15 minutes.

Makes 4 servings. PER SERVING: *Calories: 142, Protein: 2.6 g, Carbohydrates: 25.8 g, Fat: 3.5 g, % Cal. from fat: 22*

Potato Pancake

$

I recently substituted sweet potatoes in this recipe and it was just as delicious. Potato pancake makes a nice side dish for beef, lamb and poultry.

2 large potatoes, unpeeled, shredded (about ¾ pound total)
1 small onion, chopped
Salt, pepper and paprika to taste

1. Combine potatoes and onion.

2. Heat a large non-stick skillet sprayed with cooking spray. Add potato mixture, pressing it flat into a ½-inch-thick pancake. Sprinkle with salt, pepper and paprika.

3. Cook until brown on the bottom, approximately 10 minutes. Turn and cook other side 10 minutes.

Makes 4 servings. PER SERVING: *Calories: 70, Protein: 2.1 g, Carbohydrates: 15.8 g, Fat: 0.11 g, % Cal. from fat: 1*

Gingered Turnips

$

This recipe is guaranteed to make a turnip lover out of anyone who dislikes this vegetable. I often make extra and serve it cold or reheated.

1 large turnip
2 tablespoons soy sauce
1 teaspoon minced fresh ginger
1 teaspoon honey

1. Peel turnip and cut into ½-inch chunks. Place in casserole dish with ¼ cup water. Cover and cook in microwave on High for 15 minutes, turning dish and stirring turnip after 7 minutes. Drain.

2. Place turnip with remaining ingredients in food processor or blender and blend until smooth.

3. Reheat in microwave before serving.

Makes 4 servings. PER SERVING: *Calories: 42, Protein: 1.8 g, Carbohydrates: 9.3 g, Fat: 0.11 g, % Cal. from fat: 2*

Barley with Mushrooms and Onions

$ ❄

*I once made this dish with a variety of wild mushrooms (store bought!),
and it was amazing. You can double the recipe and freeze it in individual portions for those nights when you want a grain but do not have
the time to cook.*

1 large onion, chopped
½ pound fresh mushrooms, sliced
2 cups chicken broth
¾ cup barley

1. Combine onion and mushrooms in bowl with 2 tablespoons
water. Cover and cook in microwave on High for 2 minutes.

2. Pour onion and mushrooms and any liquid into pot. Add
chicken broth and barley.

3. Bring to a boil, then reduce heat to low and simmer, covered, 45 to 50 minutes, or until barley is tender and liquid is
absorbed. Stir occasionally, and add more water if necessary.

Makes 4 servings. PER SERVING: *Calories: 178, Protein: 7.8 g,
Carbohydrates: 34.8 g, Fat: 1.4 g, % Cal. from fat: 7*

Rice Pilaf

◷ $ ❄

Most recipes for rice pilaf are made with white rice. Brown rice increases both the nutrient and fibre content of this dish significantly.

1   large onion, thinly sliced
1¼ cups chicken broth
1   cup brown rice
1   tablespoon soy sauce
¾   teaspoon thyme

1. Place onions in bowl with 2 tablespoons water. Cover and cook in microwave on High for 3 minutes.

2. Combine onion with remaining ingredients in casserole dish and mix well.

3. Bake, covered, at 400°F for 40 to 50 minutes. Remove from oven and let sit at least 10 minutes before removing cover.

Makes 4 servings. PER SERVING: *Calories: 199, Protein: 5.9 g, Carbohydrates: 39.5 g, Fat: 1.7 g, % Cal. from fat: 8*

Rice and Spinach Casserole

$ ❄

This casserole can be prepared ahead of time and put in the oven 20 to 25 minutes before dinner. For added flavour, sprinkle a bit of grated Parmesan cheese on top 10 minutes before it finishes cooking.

1   cup brown rice
1   10-ounce package frozen chopped spinach, thawed and
     well drained
1   small onion, chopped
1   cup crushed canned tomatoes
1   clove garlic, minced
⅛   teaspoon pepper

1. Bring 3 cups water to a boil. Add rice, cover, and simmer 45 to 50 minutes, or until all the water is absorbed.

2. Add remaining ingredients to cooked rice and mix well.

3. Spoon rice into a casserole dish sprayed with cooking spray.

4. Bake, uncovered, at 350°F for 20 to 25 minutes.

Makes 6 servings. PER SERVING: *Calories: 136, Protein: 3.8 g, Carbohydrates: 28.5 g, Fat: 1.0 g, % Cal. from fat: 7*

Bulgur Pilaf

⊘ $ ❄

Bulgur — or cracked wheat — is a wonderful alternative to rice. It has a distinct flavour that complements beef and poultry equally well. Most health food stores carry it in bulk.

2¼ cups chicken broth
1 large onion, thinly sliced
1½ cups bulgur
1 tablespoon soy sauce
1 teaspoon thyme

1. Bring ¼ cup broth to a boil. Add onion and cook for 3 minutes.

2. Add bulgur and sauté for 3 minutes.

3. Stir in rest of the broth and remaining ingredients.

4. Pour mixture into casserole and bake, covered, at 400°F for 35 minutes. Let stand for 10 minutes before uncovering.

Makes 6 servings. PER SERVING: *Calories: 125, Protein: 6.0 g, Carbohydrates: 24.4 g, Fat: 0.96 g, % Cal. from fat: 7*

Chocolate Cupcakes

❄

Substituting cocoa powder and oil for chocolate replaces the saturated fat found in baking chocolate with polyunsaturated fat.

1¼ cups all-purpose flour
⅔ cup Splenda sweetener
⅓ cup cocoa powder
1 teaspoon baking soda
1 egg
2 egg whites
1 cup buttermilk*
¼ cup oil

1. Combine flour, sweetener, cocoa powder and baking soda in a food processor or bowl.

2. Add egg, egg whites, buttermilk and oil. Process until smooth, or blend with electric beater, about 1 minute.

3. Put 10 muffin cups in muffin tin and spray cups with cooking spray. Add batter to cups. Cups should be two-thirds full.

4. Bake at 350°F for 18 to 20 minutes, or until wooden pick inserted in centre comes out clean.

* If you don't have buttermilk, stir 1 tablespoon lemon juice into 1 cup skim milk. Let stand 5 minutes.

Makes 10 cupcakes. PER SERVING: *Calories: 133, Protein: 4.2 g, Carbohydrates: 14.6 g, Fat: 6.8 g, % Cal. from fat: 45*

Chocolate Chip Cookies

❄

This recipe, which was provided by the distributors of Splenda sweet-
ener, yields 2 dozen cookies. By making each cookie slightly smaller,
you can make 3 dozen. Smaller cookies have fewer calories. Just make
sure you don't eat twice as many.

⅓ cup softened margarine or butter
1 egg
1 teaspoon vanilla
⅔ cup Splenda sweetener
¾ cup all-purpose flour
½ teaspoon baking soda
½ cup semi-sweet chocolate chips

1. With an electric beater or in a food processor, cream margarine for 1 minute.

2. Add egg and vanilla, and blend another minute.

3. Add sweetener and blend until well mixed.

4. Combine flour and baking soda. Add to margarine mixture
and blend until smooth. Stir in chocolate chips.

5. Drop mixture from a small spoon onto an ungreased cookie sheet. Flatten slightly with back of spoon.

6. Bake at 375°F for 8 to 10 minutes, or until browned on bot-
toms.

7. Cool on rack. Store in air-tight container.

Makes 3 dozen. PER 1 COOKIE SERVING: *Calories: 38,*
Protein: 0.55 g, Carbohydrates: 3.3 g, Fat: 2.7 g, % Cal. from fat: 61

Fruit Tart

✂ ❄

For a higher-fibre, nutritious and nutty-tasting crust, I use All-Bran cereal rather than all-purpose flour. Any fruit jam can be used, but the combination of ripe strawberries and mango with President's Choice Twice the Fruit Peach and Passion Fruit Jam is amazing — a great substitute for a sugary breakfast!

Crust:
1¼ cups All-Bran cereal
¼ cup pecans
⅓ cup melted margarine or butter
2 tablespoons Splenda sweetener

Filling:
2 tablespoons cornstarch
¼ cup Splenda sweetener
1½ cups skim milk
1 egg, lightly beaten
1 teaspoon vanilla
1 pint strawberries, sliced
½ mango, sliced thinly
⅓ cup all-fruit jam

1. To make crust, process bran cereal and pecans in a food processor for 30 seconds. Transfer to small bowl and add margarine and sweetener. Mix well.

2. Press firmly into a 9-inch pie plate sprayed with cooking spray.

3. Bake at 375°F for 8 minutes, or until slightly brown at edges. Cool.

4. To make filling, combine cornstarch and sweetener in saucepan. Gradually add milk, whisking until smooth. Cook, stirring constantly, over medium heat until mixture comes to a boil.

5. Gradually whisk hot sauce into the egg and return to saucepan. Cook, stirring constantly, over low heat for 2 minutes.

6. Remove from heat. Stir in vanilla. Pour into bowl. Cover and refrigerate.

7. When chilled, pour filling into crust, spreading evenly.

8. Arrange fruit decoratively on surface. Heat jam for 1 minute in microwave or in small saucepan until melted. Brush over fruit. Chill tart until serving time.

Makes 8 servings (or 6 breakfast-sized portions). PER SERVING: *Calories: 206, Protein: 5.8 g, Carbohydrates: 27.8 g, Fat: 11 g, % Cal. from fat: 42*

Banana or Chocolate Milkshake

☉ $

The air bubbles that result from processing crushed ice and the other ingredients make these shakes filling. I find them to be a lifesaver at 4 o'clock when my blood sugar is a bit low and I crave something sweet. They keep me filled until dinnertime.

6 ice cubes
1 cup skim milk
1 small banana, sliced*
2 teaspoons Splenda sweetener
1 teaspoons vanilla

1. Process ice in blender or food processor until crushed. Scrape down sides of container.

2. Add remaining ingredients. Process until thick and frothy.

* Variation: To make a chocolate milkshake, omit banana and Splenda sweetener, and add 1 package of commercial light hot chocolate powder.

Makes 2 servings. PER SERVING: *Calories: 82, Protein: 4.6 g, Carbohydrates: 15.9 g, Fat: 0.42 g, % Cal. from fat: 4*

Carrot Cake

❄

For a more festive look, sprinkle this cake with icing sugar. You can also make the cake into 12 muffins.

2 eggs
1½ cups shredded carrot
½ cup plain low-fat yogurt
½ cup unsweetened applesauce
¼ cup oil
1 teaspoon vanilla
¾ cup all-purpose flour
¾ cup whole wheat flour
¾ cup Splenda sweetener
1½ teaspoons cinnamon
1 teaspoon baking powder
½ teaspoon baking soda
¼ teaspoon nutmeg
¼ teaspoon ginger
½ cup raisins

1. Lightly beat eggs. Stir in carrots, yogurt, applesauce, oil and vanilla.

2. In large bowl combine remaining ingredients. Add carrot mixture and stir until well blended.

3. Spread evenly in an 8-inch square cake pan sprayed with cooking spray.

4. Bake at 325°F for 35 to 40 minutes, or until wooden pick inserted in centre comes out clean. (If making muffins, bake at 400°F for 20 to 25 minutes.) Cool on rack.

Makes 12 servings or 12 muffins. PER SERVING: *Calories: 143, Protein: 3.7 g, Carbohydrates: 20.1 g, Fat: 5.8 g, % Cal. from fat: 35*

Applesauce Cake

❄

The molasses makes this applesauce cake rich and flavourful, and the applesauce makes it very moist.

1 cup all-purpose flour
1 teaspoon baking powder
½ teaspoon baking soda
2 teaspoons cinnamon
½ teaspoon ground ginger
½ cup softened, reduced-calorie margarine or butter
¼ cup molasses
1 egg
2 egg whites
1 teaspoon vanilla
1 cup Splenda sweetener
½ cup unsweetened applesauce
¼ cup chopped walnuts

1. Combine flour, baking powder, baking soda, cinnamon and ginger.

2. In large bowl with electric beater on high, cream margarine and molasses for about 1 minute.

3. Add egg, egg white and vanilla. Beat at high speed for 30 seconds. (Mixture will be very liquid.)

4. Add sweetener and beat at medium speed until smooth, about 1½ minutes.

5. Add flour mixture, applesauce and nuts. Mix well.

6. Pour batter into an 8-inch square cake pan sprayed with cooking spray. Bake at 350°F for 30 minutes, or until wooden pick inserted in centre comes out clean.

Makes 12 servings. PER SERVING: *Calories: 133, Protein: 2.6 g, Carbohydrates: 13.3 g, Fat: 7.8 g, % Cal. from fat: 52*

Peach Upside Down Cake

✂ ❄

When fresh peaches are at their peak, use them instead of the canned ones. This dessert can be served warm or cool. A tablespoon or two of plain low-fat yogurt makes a rich-tasting accompaniment.

1 tablespoon margarine or butter
¼ cup Splenda sweetener
½ teaspoon cinnamon
1 14-ounce can sliced peaches, packed in their own juice, drained
¼ cup softened margarine or butter
1 egg
1½ cups all-purpose flour
½ cup Splenda sweetener
1 teaspoon baking powder
½ teaspoon baking soda
¾ cup skim milk

1. Place 1 tablespoon margarine in a 9-inch pie plate and put in a 350°F oven to melt.

2. Combine ¼ cup sweetener and cinnamon. Sprinkle over melted margarine, which should cover bottom of pie plate. Arrange peach slices on top.

3. Cream remaining margarine with electric beater. Add egg and blend until smooth.

4. Combine flour, remaining sweetener, baking powder and baking soda.

5. Add dry ingredients and milk alternately to creamed mixture, blending until smooth after each addition.

6. Spread mixture gently over peaches. Bake at 350°F for 25 to 30 minutes, or until wooden pick inserted in centre comes out clean. Cool in pan 5 minutes and then turn out onto plate.

Makes 8 servings. PER SERVING: *Calories: 190, Protein: 4.4 g, Carbohydrates: 25.4 g, Fat: 8.0 g, % Cal. from fat: 38*

Spice Cake

❄

This spice cake makes a light dessert when served with fresh fruit on the side.

2¼ cups cake and pastry flour*
1 teaspoon baking powder
1 teaspoon baking soda
½ teaspoon nutmeg
1½ teaspoons cinnamon
½ teaspoon allspice
⅓ cup softened margarine or butter
1 egg
1 egg white
1 teaspoon vanilla
⅔ cup Splenda sweetener
1 cup plain low-fat yogurt

1. Sift together flour, baking powder, baking soda, cinnamon, nutmeg and allspice. Set aside.

2. Cream margarine with electric beater until smooth. Add egg, egg white and vanilla. Blend for 1 minute.

3. Add sweetener and blend until smooth.

4. Add flour mixture and yogurt alternately to creamed mixture, blending until smooth after each addition.

5. Pour into a 9-inch-square baking pan sprayed with cooking spray.

6. Bake at 350°F for 25 to 30 minutes, or until wooden pick inserted in centre comes out clean. Cool on rack.

*If you don't have cake and pastry flour, substitute 1 cup less 2 tablespoons all-purpose flour for each cup cake and pastry flour.

Makes 12 servings. PER SERVING: *Calories: 129, Protein: 3.3 g, Carbohydrates: 15.5 g, Fat: 5.8 g, % Cal. from fat: 41*

Lemon Chiffon Cake

❄

This cake looks extravagant, but it's not. Substituting Splenda for sugar and reducing the amount of oil found in traditional chiffon cake recipes reduces the calories by half.

2¼ cups cake and pastry flour*
1 cup Splenda sweetener
1 tablespoon baking powder
½ cup oil
2 egg yolks
¾ cup water
1½ tablespoons grated lemon rind
2 tablespoons lemon juice
8 egg whites
1 teaspoon cream of tartar

1. Sift together flour, sweetener and baking powder.

2. Make a well in centre of flour mixture. Add ingredients to well in the following order: oil, egg yolks, water, lemon rind and lemon juice. Beat with electric beater at medium speed until smooth.

3. Beat egg whites with cream of tartar until very stiff peaks form. Gently fold into batter.

4. Pour into an ungreased 10-inch tube pan or non-stick Bundt pan.

5. Bake at 325°F for 50 minutes. Invert pan and let cool for 45 minutes. Gently loosen cake from pan.

*If you don't have cake and pastry flour, substitute 1 cup less 2 tablespoons all-purpose flour for each cup cake and pastry flour.

Makes 15 servings. PER SERVING: *Calories: 134, Protein: 3.4 g, Carbohydrates: 11.7 g, Fat: 8.0 g, % Cal. from fat: 54*

Basic Bran Muffins

⏱ 💲 ❄

These easy-to-prepare muffins are also perfect for breakfast. Try them with yogurt and fruit, or with one of the shakes in this book.

1 cup skim milk
1¼ cups All-Bran cereal
¼ cup oil
1 egg
1 cup all-purpose flour
⅓ cup Splenda sweetener
2½ teaspoons baking powder
½ teaspoon baking soda
⅓ cup raisins

1. Pour milk over cereal and let sit 5 minutes. Add oil and egg. Mix well.

2. Combine remaining ingredients in a large bowl.

3. Add liquid ingredients to flour mixture and stir until just mixed. Fold in raisins.

5. Spray 12 cups of a muffin tin with cooking spray. Divide batter evenly among cups and bake at 400°F for 20 minutes.

Makes 12 small muffins. PER SERVING: *Calories: 127, Protein: 3.7 g, Carbohydrates: 19.2 g, Fat: 5.2 g, % Cal. from fat: 34*

Strawberry Muffins

❄

These muffins are an exciting change from traditional blueberry muffins.
Try them with your favourite fruit.

1 egg
1½ cups skim milk
⅓ cup oil
1 teaspoon vanilla
1¼ cups all-purpose flour
1 cup whole wheat flour
½ cup Splenda sweetener
1 tablespoon baking powder
1 teaspoon cinnamon
1 cup sliced fresh or frozen strawberries

1. Whisk together egg, milk, oil and vanilla.

2. Combine remaining ingredients, except strawberries, in large bowl.

3. Add liquid ingredients to flour mixture and stir until just mixed. Fold in strawberries.

4. Spray 12 cups of a muffin tin with cooking spray. Divide batter evenly among cups and bake at 400°F for 25 minutes.

Makes 12 muffins. PER SERVING: *Calories: 155, Protein: 4.3 g, Carbohydrates: 19.6 g, Fat: 6.8 g, % Cal. from fat: 39*

Apple Oat Muffins

❄

The combination of oat bran and apple makes these muffins a good source of soluble fibre.

1½ cups oat bran
½ cup whole wheat flour
⅓ cup Splenda sweetener
2 teaspoons baking powder
1 teaspoon cinnamon
1 cup peeled, cored and diced apples
½ cup apple juice
¼ cup skim milk
1 egg, lightly beaten
3 tablespoons oil

1. Combine oat bran, flour, sweetener, baking powder, and cinnamon.

2. Combine remaining ingredients in separate bowl.

3. Add liquid ingredients to dry, stirring until just moistened.

4. Spray 12 cups of a muffin tin with cooking spray. Divide batter evenly among cups and bake at 400°F for 20 minutes.

Makes 12 muffins. PER SERVING: *Calories: 90, Protein: 3.1 g, Carbohydrates: 13.0 g, Fat: 4.6 g, % Cal. from fat: 39*

INDEX